Moving Forward

Life After Trauma

Stephanie M. Hutchins, PhD

Dedication

To those who feel, or have felt,
they are trapped by their unchangeable past.

Table of Contents

Introduction

What Is Trauma?

L ike many others who've experienced trauma, I used to be inflamed by phrases like, "You've gotta move on" or "You gotta move forward." Early in my life when my traumas were at their worst, I wanted to scream, "But you have no idea what I've gone through!" I was enraged at the ignorance or disregard for the pain I endured.

Even as I started to heal, I wanted to put my head down in defeat when I heard those phrases, frustrated by the enormity of what they were suggesting. It seemed impossible. I always thought, How can I move past what I experienced — every form of sexual violations, from multiple men, starting at a young age? How can I move past having someone come up behind me and put a knife to my throat? How can I move past finding the first man who made me feel I was deserving of love and respect dead? I just wished they would tell me how. But no one seemed to know. They would just spout the little bit of knowledge and understanding they had of trauma, which always culminated in some version of "Just get over it."

Given the little appreciation I have for the times I've been told to "Just move on," you may find it odd that I chose to use the words "moving forward" in the title of this book. It's, of course, on purpose. I feel like this message is on replay in various shapes and forms in the lives of all of us who've experienced trauma, with very little, if any, explanation for how to even accomplish that task. It usually comes from people who want us to stop making them uncomfortable when we share our stories of suffering, who've never experienced trauma, or who are just parroting the same destructive messages they heard after their own traumatic experience.

After our world shatters, we often ask questions such as: How do I pick up the broken pieces? How do I mend the jagged edges back together? How do I move through the world after tragedy strikes, knowing my life will never be the same, even though I wish that wasn't true? This book is designed to answer these questions and many more.

To begin answering these questions, I'll start by saying that not a single step in the process is simple or easy. The process is messy and will last longer and typically be more painful than the trauma you endured. However, it is crucial for you to know that it's possible to reach the holy grail of moving forward after your trauma. As misguided as most might be when they use such phrases as "Just move on," it is possible to achieve the difficult task of taking steps to separate yourself from your pain. Once you begin taking those initial steps forward, you'll be able to start the process of envisioning a life for yourself that isn't based on the version of you that was marred by your trauma.

For years, I felt like I was part of the walking dead. I thought my life had ended at the moment my traumas began and that the remainder of my life would be spent struggling to survive. But that wasn't the case! Instead of just merely surviving after my traumas, I thrived! Something that I previously thought was impossible became my new reality. Now I'm dedicating my life to help others reclaim their lives after trauma.

Between my live workshops, online courses, coaching clients, social media followers, email subscribers, and the readers of my books, I get a lot of questions about healing from trauma. What I've begun to see is a trend in the questions I'm asked. These questions and the emerging trends inspired this book. In the coming chapters, I'll answer the questions I get asked the most about healing from trauma.

Even though I have a PhD, I'm not a licensed clinician and this book isn't filled with research. The responses to the questions are based on my own trauma history; what I've learned from my healing journey; what I've learned from the years I spent studying and teaching about the human body and mind; and what I've learned from working with others who've experienced trauma.

Let's begin with a question I get asked on many podcast interviews: What is trauma? The American Psychological Association defines trauma as:

Any disturbing experience that results in significant fear, helplessness, dissociation, confusion, or other disruptive feelings intense enough to have a long-lasting negative effect on a person's attitudes, behavior, and other aspects of functioning. Traumatic events include those caused by human behavior (e.g., rape, war, industrial accidents) as well as by nature (e.g., earthquakes) and often challenge an individual's view of the world as a just, safe, and predictable place.[1]

When I discuss trauma, I'm referring to the event itself but with the understanding that the event triggered a cascade of psychological responses. The psychological responses to the event are what determines whether the event will be perceived as traumatic by the individual. This variation in psychological responses is why the same event might be traumatic to one person but not another. The key is whether the event challenged the individual's ability to cope once the event was over. One's ability to cope after experiencing a distressing event depends on the person's life experiences prior to the event and the coping skills and support systems they had in place after the event.

For some people, the event may have reinforced negative beliefs they already had about themselves or life. This can send a person into a downward spiral of self-loathing and hopelessness, where they don't see a way out of their pain. Whereas another person may experience the same event but don't internalize it as having a deeper meaning about themself, the type of person they are, or about the world they live in. If a person experiences a distressing event without having ever been shown ways of coping with extremely stressful situations or without having people in their life to lean on during the aftermath of the event, it may ingrain in the individual that they're never going to be able to handle this event and that they're going to feel this deep level of pain for the rest of their life. Whereas another person could experience the same event but have the coping skills, were provided the resources, and had people to lean on after they experienced the painful event. A person who is provided mechanisms to cope isn't going to keep cycling through the painful experience for as long as a person who doesn't have the skills, resources, or people available to help them get through it.

What all trauma has in common is that it overwhelms your internal capacity to cope. It has made you feel hopeless and at a loss of control. Oftentimes, a traumatic event is considered to be a catastrophic event like war, sexual or physical assault, or a severe car accident. While I do believe these are traumatic events, I also believe that given a certain set of life circumstances, stressful life events can be traumatic as well. Loss of a job or divorce are considered stressful events, but in and of themselves, they're not usually considered traumatic. But let's say your parents got divorced when you were a child, and you blame yourself for your father no longer wanting to be in your life. You were able to cope with life after that, but there was always this lingering sense of self-doubt. Then your husband asks for a divorce. This could be life altering, if you still believe you're unlovable and unworthy from when your father left. The divorce could then become a traumatic event in your life.

Or, let's say you were constantly bullied in high school. You were able to make it through, you go to college, you pursue your chosen career, and then you get fired. A job loss would typically be considered a stressful event and not traumatic. However, when you compound the feelings of inadequacy that may follow job loss with the feelings of something being "wrong with you" from your years of being bullied, the job loss can suddenly catapult you into a downward spiral you can't seem to dig yourself out of.

For these reasons, I don't qualify different types of traumas as being worse than others. I do think it's important to have perspective when thinking about your trauma, but you must be careful not to minimize your pain. Yes, someone will always have it worse than you, but another person's experience is irrelevant to your own. If you were raped by a boyfriend, it isn't helpful to think, *Well, at least I wasn't gang raped.* Yet, that's exactly how many of us feel, or other people make us feel. For you, that was likely the worst thing you've ever experienced, and to minimize it by saying it could have been worse can be very disheartening. It can make you feel guilty for feeling the thoughts you do. It can make you feel ashamed your experiences were debilitating when others who've faced similar or "worse" have recovered. What must be taken into consideration are the internal and external resources you have available to you before, during, and after your trauma. Previous life experiences must be taken into consideration.

It breaks my heart to see someone feel guilty or ashamed for letting their trauma alter their life because they're focusing on others who they think have had to deal with so much worse. Someone else's reality is not your own. Minimizing your feelings, thoughts, or emotions because you think your trauma isn't as bad as somebody else's isn't healthy or useful, because their reality is not your reality. It just makes you feel worse. Here you've been traumatized but feel like you shouldn't still feel sad or hurt, because you think your experiences weren't as bad as somebody else's. You're not being empathetic, kind, or compassionate to yourself if you say that you can't feel a certain way because you didn't experience a certain level of trauma. You shouldn't base any of your feelings on whether your reality is as good or as bad as somebody else's reality.

That's why I use the word "trauma" to encompass all events, or a group of events, that have challenged one's ability to cope. What may cause low levels of stress in one person, may send another into a complete tailspin based on their life circumstances. I also don't like to use phrases like "big-T trauma" and "little-t trauma." I see it all the time; the sheer shame and disappointment people feel by still being held back by a "little-t trauma." Even when they don't use that term, that's what they are doing. They'll say, "I haven't had it nearly as bad as you have," or "I know some people have it much worse than I do." They're minimizing their pain, and that keeps them stuck.

I encourage you to evaluate whether you've done this yourself. Awareness is the key to making any change. So, it's important to acknowledge whether there is part of you that doesn't feel you have any right to suffer or to be suffering for as long as you have been. If part of you feels this way, there is no doubt in my mind that it's keeping you stuck. How on Earth can you move beyond your pain, if you don't believe you should be in pain in the first place? You can't!

Part of my job as a life coach is to help my clients move from an unresourceful state to a resourceful state. Unresourceful states are also known as "stuck states" because they make you feel as though the way you're currently feeling is inescapable, and that you don't have choices at that moment. A resourceful state is where you feel capable and comfortable in your body and in control of your circumstances. Your mind can generate options, make decisions, and allow you to effectively respond to your environment. One way many people keep themselves stuck in an unresourceful state is with the way they talk to themselves.

Although the primary focus of this book is to provide answers to common questions about healing from trauma, it'll be like my other books in that it also includes action items so you can immediately apply the information to your own life and make change. That's why I encourage you to get a journal to use while reading this book.

In addition to using the journal for the activities in this book, I encourage you to make notes about any new insights you've received while moving through this book. Did something cause you to think or feel a different way? If so, write it down. I also encourage you to use your journal to write about difficult thoughts or feelings that come up while reading this book or in daily life to get them out of your system. If you're concerned about others reading your private thoughts, I encourage you to get a journal that locks, use a password-protected journaling app like Penzu, or write on individual sheets of paper and shred them afterward. But it's essential to get your thoughts out of your system and not hold them in where they can fester and wreak havoc.

Let's begin with our first journaling activity.

Activity

Get out your journal and answer the following questions:
- Have you ever minimized your pain? If yes, how? For example, talking about how someone else has had it worse than you.
- Have you ever condemned yourself for "still" suffering? If yes, how? For example, have you thought that you should "be over it by now"?
- Have you ever criticized yourself for the ways you've tried to survive? If yes, how? For example, have you condemned yourself because you overate, drank too much alcohol, used drugs, or engaged in casual sex?

If you answered yes to any of these questions, then you've trapped yourself in a cycle of negative thoughts. If you haven't yet gotten yourself out of this trap, then it'll be important for you to work on changing that narrative so you can move yourself into a resourceful state where you have options for moving through and beyond your pain. To do this, you must first acknowledge that you experienced pain, what you experienced was hard, and that other people's experiences are irrelevant to your own. It's your pain, and for you, it was hard; and that's all that matters.

Next, you'll need to show yourself empathy and compassion for what you've endured. You must acknowledge that your pain is being caused by so much more than the traumatic events themselves; all the hurtful words, actions, or inactions of others have compounded to make your most painful experiences even worse. It's how it plays out in our minds and in our bodies long after the trauma occurred that really wreaks havoc in our life. Trauma can infiltrate every aspect of our lives, from our careers, finances, and health, to our relationships with ourselves and others. So be kind to yourself and acknowledge that you've suffered and been doing the best you can to survive in the aftermath.

It's good that many countries are becoming more open to addressing trauma and mental health issues. For years, we were all supposed to walk around pretending we're never in pain, but the reality is that most of us are in immense pain. Even though many societies are now more open to addressing mental health issues, most of us still stuff down our sadness into the deepest recesses within and pretend it doesn't exist. But little by little, our sadness eats away at us, and that pain infiltrates every aspect of our life.

Thankfully, more people are starting to acknowledge how we pass our pain along to others. We perpetuate generational trauma because we aren't addressing our pain. Instead, we push it away and put a smile on our face just to make sure we don't make anyone around us uncomfortable. But it creates immense pressure inside when we hold on to our pain. That's why many people lash out with hurtful words and actions when they're in pain. Their pain never went anywhere.

By continuing to pretend our pain from the past no longer exists and the pain we face in our present life is no big deal, we end up feeling ready to burst from the buildup of years of hurt. Eventually, it becomes too much to contain, so we discharge it in any way we can. Usually, by spewing it all over others. People who don't discharge their pain onto the world, usually aim their pain back at themselves and begin to self-destruct through actions like overeating, drinking, using drugs, or engaging in casual sex. Some people do both: project their pain outwardly and inwardly.

As you move through this book and complete the activities, I encourage you to think about how you'll be able to change the way you experience life when you stop allowing your trauma to steal your life from you. I encourage you to think about how it'll change how you interact with others and reduce the likelihood that you'll hurt others when you can move through and beyond your pain. By minimizing your pain and condemning yourself for "still" suffering and all the ways you've tried to survive, you won't be able to complete the cycle of processing your trauma. You'll get stuck at the same place over and over when you think about your trauma.

My hope is that as you move through this book and receive answers to your questions and tools for breaking old patterns, you'll be able to move into the life you desire and deserve. Not a life that is shackled to your unchangeable past.

Chapter 1

Will I Ever Forget?

Whenever I get the question, "Will I ever forget my trauma?", I sense how desperate the person is to hear, "Yes, there will come a day when you'll stop remembering." Unfortunately, I can't give them that answer. The reality is that we never forget our trauma. I liken it to a spider web with its sticky silk and the spider that wraps its prey with this same sticky substance. Our traumas stick to us and envelope us in the same way.

On August 19, 2021, I participated in the workshop, Trauma & the Journey to Wholeness: Art Making and Healing, led by Sheryl Kaplan and Judith Prest at the Wiawaka Center for Women, in Lake George, New York. One of the day's activities was to use some art form to tell our story. I chose to collage on storyboards the different stages of moving through and beyond my suffering.

On my first storyboard, I had a big spider web and multiple spiders. This represented the period during my childhood and early teens when I was violated numerous times by different men. The spiders represented the men crawling over my body; the unwanted touching. The spider web represented how what they did to me is still stuck to me. As an avid hiker, I regularly walk through spider webs. The memories of what these men did to me stick like those spider webs. No matter how much I shake my hands and try to get it off me, it just stays stuck to me even though the spiders that made the web are gone. Even though the men who hurt me decades ago are gone, the memories of what they did to me are still stuck to me like a spider web.

The effects of trauma are so much bigger than the event itself with how the memories of the event and the psychological aftereffects invade every aspect of our life after the trauma is over. Because the memories of our trauma follow us wherever we go, they can easily creep in and invade every aspect of our life. This is why trauma is so devastating and can make us feel trapped.

We'll never be able to forget our trauma because our brain will never allow us to forget. As psychiatrist Dr. Mark Goulston says, "Unlike simple stress, trauma changes your view of your life and yourself. It shatters your most basic assumptions about yourself and your world — 'Life is good,' 'I'm safe,' 'People are kind,' 'I can trust others,' 'The future is likely to be good' — and replaces them with feelings like 'The world is dangerous,' 'I can't win,' 'I can't trust other people,' or 'There's no hope.'"[2]

Our brain has developed to protect us. We remember when we experience something painful, so our brain can look out for similar dangers in the future to decrease the likelihood of us getting hurt in a similar way again. Even if there are components of our trauma that we can't remember consciously, our subconscious mind stores our experiences. That's why those who have blocked out childhood trauma may engage in self-destructive behaviors for apparently no reason or experience a variety of mental or physical health issues even though they don't consciously remember the traumatic event. Their subconscious mind has stored the memories.

Although it may feel disheartening that we'll never be able to forget our trauma, it's important to first face that fact head on so you can stop resisting it. We're fighting a losing battle when we expend energy on resentment for our traumas and wish we would forget so we can move on with our life. We can't undo any portion of our past, even though we'll forever carry around the memories from our unchangeable past. This book isn't just about giving you information, it's about shifting the way you look at your past so you can move through and beyond your pain. It's about getting you unstuck. Sometimes to get unstuck, we need to stand still long enough to fully assess our situation, including what we do and do not have control over.

Activity

Get out your journal and write down how you feel about the fact that you'll never be able to forget your trauma. The purpose of this activity isn't to bring you into your pain and keep you there. It's also not about making you feel bad and ruminate over what you've lost and what will no longer be because of your trauma. That's why I'm not encouraging you to write about the details of your trauma and the devastation that's been left behind. For this activity, you're specifically focusing on the thoughts and feelings you have about never being able to forget your trauma.

In case you begin to feel sad, angry, or any other difficult emotion while completing this activity, any coming activity, or in life in general, also write some comforting things you can say to yourself when you're upset. Is there something someone said to you in the past that helped? Is there something you wish someone else had said to you in the past? If so, write it down and say it out loud to yourself. This is about honoring the part of you that's in pain. It's about empathizing with your wounded inner child and providing yourself with the love and compassion you need to begin moving beyond your pain.

The purpose of this book is to show you that you can continue to move forward with your life even though you've experienced immense suffering. It's about building up your arsenal to fight memories, as well as difficult thoughts, feelings, and emotions associated with your trauma. Having something kind and compassionate to say to yourself when you're in pain can be helpful in preventing you from staying stuck in a difficult emotion for long.

Unfortunately, trying to figure out how to move forward after our trauma is usually much more difficult than experiencing the trauma itself. That's why it's easy for people to get stuck after their trauma. It's easy to get frustrated by how the trauma always follows us around and feel like we'll always suffer because of it. If you're in this place, please know that over time the memories of your trauma will revisit you less and less. Eventually, the memories will become easier to manage when they do resurface. Most important and uplifting is knowing that, in time, you'll have the ability to use the memories of your suffering to your advantage. These topics will be covered in later chapters.

Because we'll never forget our trauma, we must find a way to navigate our life knowing that the most painful experiences we've endured will always be part of us. That's why we must figure out a way to handle the memories when they resurface. The purpose of the next chapter is to give you the tools to do just that.

Chapter 2

How Can I Handle Being Triggered?

Because we'll always carry around memories of our trauma, there will always be things that trigger us to remember the most painful experiences of our life. It may be certain smells, songs, words, looks, or actions by another person. As psychiatrist Dr. Judith Lewis Herman says, "After a traumatic experience, the human system of self-preservation seems to go on permanent alert, as if the danger might return at any moment."[3] This means our subconscious mind is always looking out for potential danger, even when we're not conscious of it. This means moments of joy can be unexpectedly stolen from us, even if our trauma occurred many years ago. I experienced this during a trip to Letchworth State Park in New York in May 2022.

The trip to Letchworth started out beautifully. On our way, my friend and I stopped at Watkins Glen State Park, where we had a magnificent walk past the 19 waterfalls in the park, and I was saying, "Wow" everywhere we looked because it was so beautiful. When we arrived at Letchworth, we checked into the cute little cabin we rented for the weekend. However, when we drove up to it, I noticed that most of the people outside the other cabins were men drinking. Then, when I was walking to the bathroom, which was in a separate building, an older gentleman also walking toward the bathroom commented that we weren't likely going to get a lot of sleep tonight with this rowdy bunch.

Shortly after arriving, I went from feeling great and blessed for the beautiful day, to feeling afraid. By the time I got to the bathroom, thoughts of all the places a man could be hiding had already injected me with fear and knew I needed to be on the lookout when going to the bathroom at night. In the bathroom, I could hear the men talking and laughing outside and knew they would just get more boisterous as the night went on, because it was only about 4:00 p.m. at that time.

My hypervigilance just increased from there. When I walked out of the bathroom, I could feel my heart race and chest tighten as I tried to determine all the different directions I could be attacked from between the bathroom and my cabin. As I looked around to assess the situation, I noticed that my friend and I were the only women currently visible in this isolated section of the campground, and there were about 30 men outside. My heart beat faster, and my chest tightened further as I planned how to minimize my trips to the bathroom and how to barricade the door to our cabin each night. All this processing occurred in the span of about five minutes. It's astonishing how quickly my beautiful part of the day was stolen from me as my brain went on high alert. My joy vanished as my mind recalled all the times I had been sexually violated by men, particularly by men who had been drinking, and the time a man came up behind me and put a knife to my throat.

Sometimes when I'm triggered, like at the campground, it makes perfect sense. Sometimes it doesn't. I can be walking and looking at the trees moving with the wind or doing work on my computer completely unrelated to trauma and have a flashback, which is another post-traumatic stress disorder (PTSD) symptom I still experience from time to time when triggered. Sometimes the flashbacks come in my dreams or when I watch a movie that has scenes like what I experienced. To combat this potentially debilitating PTSD symptom, I've developed ways to cope when I'm re-experiencing a past trauma in my mind, which I will cover later in this section. However, I do what I can to minimize how often I'm triggered, based on my known triggers.

I know that watching or hearing someone being raped, or about to be, will always trigger me. It's become an important practice for me to google whether movies have rape scenes so I can avoid watching the movie if it does. For example, I'll type into Google, "Does ____ movie have rape scenes," and the search results will tell me if it does or not. My mind catalogs every rape scene I've ever seen or heard. So even if I close my eyes, plug my ears, and even leave the room, I maintain a vivid memory of what I did see and hear. What's been most unexpected in my healing journey is how vividly I remember the victimization of others. I get the same visceral reaction and replaying of scenes in my mind when I remember others being raped as I do to my own sexual violations.

Another PTSD symptom I experience is an exaggerated startle response. I feel like I'm going to jump out of my skin if someone comes up behind me when I didn't realize they were there. For a while afterward, I can feel my heart racing and a sense of panic as my body adjusts to what it thought was the near miss of another attack.

Like many others who have experienced trauma, I also suffer from chronic physical pain, particularly in my back, as my muscles are always preparing to fight or run away from danger. Many of my muscles are tight and contain palpable knots from my body always being primed for action. I also struggle with extreme anxiety and panic attacks, also common PTSD symptoms, which make the physical pain worse.

Even though I've made a tremendous amount of progress in my healing journey, there will continue to be times when my past creeps in and rips me out of the present moment and brings me back to my past. It's difficult to not get discouraged during these times, but I must always remind myself that that's part of the trauma healing journey. We'll never forget our trauma, so we must find ways to cope and deal with it when it creeps back into our present life. Even if our past trauma steals present moments of joy from us, we can take steps to prevent our past from derailing us and keeping us stuck in the past for hours or days.

Not everyone who has experienced trauma develops PTSD, and not everyone who develops PTSD will experience all its possible symptoms. Regardless of whether you have PTSD or not, and regardless of what triggers you to remember your past trauma, it's important to have a plan in place to remain in the present moment so you don't get catapulted into your past.

Whenever I'm triggered and my PTSD symptoms flare up, I focus on my breathing. Changing our breathing is something we always have control over, we can change it regardless of the circumstances. It anchors us in the present and is the quickest way to change our body's physical response to stress. When focusing on my breathing, I breathe slowly and deeply with my belly and remind myself that I'm safe at this moment. Sometimes when my thoughts begin to race, my heart beats faster, and I feel my chest tighten. I want to cry because of the level of overwhelm I'm feeling at that moment, but I usually force myself not to, because crying usually makes me spiral down even further, and I'm more likely to get stuck in my feeling of overwhelm.

Instead, I continue to breathe deeply and remind myself that I'm safe. Then I work on coming back to a single point of focus. It may be my breath. If I'm triggered while working, my point of focus is the project I'm working on. If I'm on a walk, my point of focus may be on putting one step in front of the other, feeling the breeze on my skin, or watching the trees sway or birds fly.

That's why I've found meditation to be helpful and will cover it further later in this section, because it's all about training your mind to come back to a single point of focus each time your mind gets pulled off course. If I'm watching a movie that triggers me, I'll either walk away or mute the TV and close my eyes until the scene is over. If I wake up at night from a bad dream, I turn on the TV, music, or an audiobook to allow my focus to be brought to something else.

Because PTSD is an anxiety disorder, I've found medication to be helpful in controlling my anxiety. I resisted medication for years. I felt it meant I was weak, and I felt I should be able to control my anxiety on my own. There are still times today that I'm resentful for needing to take medication to control my emotions. It's during these times that I must remember that trauma causes short-term and long-term changes in our brain chemistry and structure, and medication can help combat these changes and make the symptoms more manageable. If your doctor wants you to try medication for your trauma symptoms, but you're also hesitant, I encourage you to keep this in mind. Trying to change the fact that your trauma altered how your brain works, won't do anything to normalize your brain function; it'll only make you more dysregulated and increase the severity of your trauma symptoms.

Medication can help decrease our need for unhealthy coping mechanisms like overeating, drinking, using drugs, cutting, or engaging in casual sex. All these coping mechanisms release the chemicals in our brain we're looking for to stabilize our feelings and emotions. By taking medication that gives us the chemicals we need to regulate our emotions, we're less likely to become dysregulated and feel so out of control that we turn to an unhealthy coping strategy.

Over recent years, I've taken citalopram daily. The dose I take depends on what's going on in my life at the time. Stressful times in my life make my PTSD symptoms worse. It becomes a vicious cycle. When I'm experiencing hyperarousal and my body and mind go on high alert, it exacerbates the stress in my life, which continues to worsen my PTSD symptoms. During those times of high stress, I take more medication to regulate the overexaggerated stress response in my body. This sometimes includes me taking Xanax or propranolol to lessen the physical signs of anxiety. When I experience severe panic attacks, I can still feel my heart beating faster and tightness in my chest even after taking these medications. It's during these times that healthy coping strategies like going for a walk, calling a friend, or practicing deep breathing are critical.

That's the thing with taking medication — it doesn't negate the need for positive coping strategies. People think they can pop a pill and it'll make all their negative emotions go away, but it doesn't work like that. There is work you must do to get yourself back into emotional balance.

Another thing I do when I can feel myself spiraling downward is make sure to tell other people how I'm feeling. In the instance in the campground, I told my friend what was happening. When I'm by myself, I'll call a family member or friend and tell them what is happening. This has been a big step in my healing journey because I previously would have gone inward and stayed there, but now I see other people as resources to help pull me out of a hole or prevent me from going in the hole in the first place. Building resources, both internal and external, is key to healing from trauma and dealing with the ways our trauma will forever live in our mind and body. It's essential to help us differentiate between what's happening in the present versus what happened in the past, because, when we're triggered, it can be difficult to tell the difference. The point of this book is not just to answer your questions, but also to give you tools to build your arsenal to handle the moments when your past tries to take over your present life.

All we ever have is this one moment. That's all life is — a progression from one moment to the next. So, if we're experiencing joy in this one moment, we must do whatever we can to hold on to it, and if past pain is trying to steal our present joy from us, we must do whatever we can to stop it. As you know, trauma steals so much from us. It steals huge swaths of our life. Trauma is so much more than the event itself; it infiltrates every aspect of our life long after the event. We must do whatever we can to minimize the way trauma drains life from us. We can't do anything about the fact that we experienced trauma and the past our trauma has already stolen from us, but we can take steps to minimize further theft of the life we have left. The next activity will give you the opportunity to develop ways to stop your past from stealing more life from you in the present and in the future.

Activity

In this activity, you'll identify your triggers, what happens in your mind and body when you're triggered, and what you can do when you're triggered. It'll be easiest to complete this activity if you print out the Handle Being Triggered worksheet. You can access this worksheet at *serotinouslife.com/worksheets.* However, if you don't currently have access to a printer, you can use your journal to record your responses. If using your journal, make three columns on the page. Title the first column Causes, the second Signs and Symptoms, and the third Interventions.

To complete the chart, fill out the first column, Causes. Write down everything you know that triggers you. Is it people saying certain things to you? Is it seeing or smelling certain things? Is it going to certain places or into certain spaces?

Then move on to the Signs and Symptoms column and write down everything that happens in your mind and body when you're triggered. Does your heart race or chest feel tight? Do you feel sick to your stomach? Does your low back start to ache, or do the muscles between your shoulder blades tense? Do you feel sad, depressed, frustrated, or angry? Does your mind race, or do you feel that you're going to lose control?

In the Interventions column, write down what you can do when you're triggered to prevent the signs and symptoms from showing up or to stop them from escalating. Could you say the comforting words you wrote down in the activity in Chapter 1? If the trigger involves another person, how could you vocalize your needs? Could you go for a walk, take a bath, listen to music, call a friend, spend a few minutes watching a funny clip on YouTube, play a game, or do a puzzle? Could you change your breathing by taking deep belly breaths?

Changing our breathing pattern is the quickest way to change our state and calm our stress response. The great thing is that we have control over our breathing and can change it anytime, regardless of the circumstances. Belly breathing, also known as diaphragmatic breathing, is particularly beneficial because it allows you to maximize your oxygen intake and release the maximum amount of waste from your lungs. In addition, if you force yourself to breathe with your belly, you're signaling to your brain that you're okay. If you can focus on consciously breathing with your belly, it must mean you're not in danger, and your fight-or-flight response will calm down. At that point, your heart rate and breathing can slow, allowing the tension in your muscles to subside.

To practice belly breathing, place one or both hands on your stomach. Slowly inhale through your nose and let your belly expand. Slowly exhale through your mouth and feel your belly come back in. So, the pattern is: belly goes out with each inhale and in with each exhale. If you've never practiced this before, it'll feel strange and difficult at first, that's why you must practice this breathing pattern ahead of time before you need it.

If you need additional ideas for self-care practices to handle the moments when you're triggered, I encourage you to read or listen to my book, *Transformation After Trauma: Embracing Post-Traumatic Growth*, where I provide detailed instructions for the different self-care tools I used in my healing journey.

Typically, physical signs of stress show up before you're aware you're under stress. That's why it's important to begin scanning yourself for physical signs of stress the moment you experience something that would typically put you on high alert. Once you become aware of your body's stress signals, immediately implement at least one intervention strategy. The good thing about the interventions you chose for this activity is that they can be used anytime you experience stress, not just when you're triggered to remember your past trauma.

Also try to combine intervention strategies. For example, you can combine saying comforting words to yourself while you're doing belly breathing or on a walk. Not all interventions will be accessible in every instance you're triggered. So, you want to have a variety of tools to choose from. You also want to be open to trying new tools so that if one strategy isn't working, you can try something else.

Regardless of the intervention strategies you choose, it's important to practice them ahead of time. Defaulting to belly breathing or vocalizing your needs won't happen if you don't practice them before you need them. You must practice these interventions before your brain and body are on high alert. You may not be able to think as clearly when you're triggered, so you need your tools to be accessible when you're spiraling down the rabbit hole. This may involve you practicing belly breathing for one to two minutes each day. It may involve you finding one way to speak up for yourself each day in an instance where you wouldn't have before. Whatever you choose for your intervention strategies, find ways to practice using them regularly so your brain will reach for them as options when you're triggered.

I've had people ask me why their flashbacks and panic attacks are worse sometimes than others. I experience this phenomenon myself. What I've found is that when my fight-or-flight response is stimulated, I'm more likely to experience flashbacks. Our fight-or-flight response can be triggered by multiple kinds of stressors, like stress at work, stress with family and friends, or stress at school. PTSD is caused by an overreaction of the fight-or-flight response. There is an imbalance of chemicals being released in the brain. So, when you begin stimulating this release of chemicals through a stress response, it can create further imbalances, causing you to go back in your mind and body into previous traumatic experiences. That's why, if you're not currently working with a medical professional as part of your trauma healing journey, I encourage you to do so. There are a lot of self-care activities that can help with decreasing the overreaction of the nervous system, but if it's really severe and impeding your ability to function, healthcare professionals can prescribe medication to help regulate the chemicals and get you back into balance. Not everyone likes to reach for medications, but if your physical experiences are linked to a dysregulation of chemicals in the brain, then medication can help rebalance those chemicals. However, as I've said before, even with medication, you must still practice self-care. It's also important to work with a medical professional in your healing journey, particularly when your symptoms flare up and especially if you're having suicidal thoughts.

In times when trauma symptoms are high, it's important to come at them with everything you can. That's why it's important to build your arsenal so you have multiple ways to attack the symptoms of stress when you're healing and when you're triggered. When life bears down on you, you must come back at it with everything you've got.

I've found meditation to be particularly helpful in working through times when I'm triggered. I choose a point of focus, typically my breath, and focus on it for a minute or two. Although meditation is a powerful way to improve your life and help you through your healing journey, it can be scary to practice, especially when you're just beginning. When we experience trauma, we often avoid being in silence. We avoid being still. We're scared that scenes from our past will come up and we won't know how to handle it. But that's exactly why meditation is so powerful. It proves to us that painful thoughts can arise, and we have the power to let them go. It allows us to stay present and know that was then and this is now.

Meditation is about training our mind to come back to a single point of focus, like our breath, each time we get off track. There will always be things that pull us off track like negative thoughts, people, and circumstances. Meditation is called a practice because we will always get off track; that's how our mind and life work. It takes constant practice to come back to our point of focus, whether that is our breath, our work, or listening to the person we are talking to at the moment.

Whenever memories from your past creep in, it's important to remember that if you survived the event you can survive the memory. They're just memories. Although they may feel real, they're not real. That's why it's important to do whatever you can to bring yourself back to the present moment and remind yourself that nothing is happening to you at this moment. It's only a memory.

We get so scared of going back and remembering but forget that we already survived, and the event is over. Yes, I understand that it's scary not knowing when you'll be triggered and for how long you'll stay immersed in memories of your trauma. As you build your arsenal, you'll build confidence in being able to handle the moments when you're triggered, and your fear of being triggered will decrease. Again, this is why meditation is so powerful; it allows you to practice coming back to your single point of focus, even if a terrible memory is trying to intrude. Over time, you'll see that a painful memory can come to mind, and you can choose to not let it get you off track by choosing to not focus on it.

Although there will always be things that make us remember our trauma, the frequency of those memories will decrease over time. The more time that passes and the more work you do on yourself, the less often you'll be triggered. I've found it helpful to think about what Brianna Wiest said about taking triggers as signals. In her book, *The Mountain Is You*, she said, "Triggers are not random; they are showing you where you are either most wounded or primed for growth."[4] This has helped me because like most trauma survivors, I used to be afraid of being triggered and would do anything to prevent it, because I didn't know if I could handle the onslaught of memories that may or may not follow. Starting to think about triggers as helpful allowed me to reframe how I thought about being triggered. Over time, I was able to look with curiosity at the times I was triggered. I looked at them as opportunities to determine what additional work I needed to do in my healing. Each time I delve a little deeper into exploring my wounds, I get stronger. The only way we can patch a wound is by getting close to it. Each time I'm made aware of where my past wounds still need tending to, I can take steps to allow them to heal. Not only do I get stronger because I allow a damaged part of me to heal, but the process of journeying inward allows me to get stronger. The hold our trauma has on us shrivels when we look at it in a new way. This is why we'll be discussing the importance of reframing in trauma healing later in this book.

I know in the early stages of our grief it can seem that our trauma will consume the rest of our life, but that's not the case. It'll always be part of us, but we don't have to let it dictate our future and the way we experience life going forward. Although you may not have been in control when you experienced your trauma, you are in control now. I know it may not feel that way when your past creeps into your mind, but you are. They're just memories. They're not the actual event. Calling them out for what they are, just memories, puts you in control. It's empowering, the moment you realize you can practice the control you didn't have during your trauma by practicing control over how you handle the moments when your past keeps trying to steal bits of your present life from you.

How Can I Handle Dissociation?

For much of my life, I've looked at birds with envy. I've coveted their ability to fly away at any time. The closest I've gotten is through dissociating — the act of disconnecting from one's surroundings. I've only experienced dissociation while being sexually assaulted, but not, unfortunately, during each assault or throughout the entire assault. I'm thankful for this but frustrated by it at the same time. I'm grateful my brain provided me with a way to escape during some assaults, but when I would come in and out of the dissociative state during the assaults, it left me with fragmented memories. I can only remember snippets of some of the experiences. This has been particularly difficult for me to handle with the memories from my earliest victimization.

I estimate that my first experiences with sexual abuse began when I was nine years old. But I could have been younger. I determined the age of nine as an adult when I understood the timeline of events going on during that period in my life. I also have no idea how long the abuses occurred for. The memories only come to me in pieces. When these memories started coming to me later in life, it made me doubt the truth of what I was remembering. As I remembered more, some memories became more vivid. As I put them together with experiences I had with the same person as I got older, I knew for sure that I was abused by this person, but even today, I still get frustrated that I can't remember everything. Even though I know the abuse happened, not being able to remember all the details gives me a feeling like I dreamt it all up. That always fills me with a sense of doubt. It helped when my therapist told me I was unlikely to make up a story of being sexually abused by a family member as a child. It's more likely that it happened, and I just can't remember all the pieces.

The biology professor in me knows it doesn't make any sense that children would make up stories about being sexually violated, especially by a family member, someone they were supposed to be able to trust. As children, we depend on the adults around us to keep us safe. It doesn't make sense that we would default to stories of them making us unsafe unless that's what really happened. But because our views of the world are still being formed as children, abuse during those formative years can be unbearable for a developing brain, which is why children are less likely to remember the abuses they've endured. Their brain allowed them to dissociate, to leave their body and mind and go somewhere else while they were being hurt, or to see the abuse happening to someone other than themselves.

There have been times I've wished I could will myself to dissociate, but I couldn't. When I had boyfriends back me into a corner, yelling at me and belittling me while they towered over me, I would will my brain to take me away, but it didn't. Sometimes, I would be in the passenger seat of the car, and my boyfriend would be viciously yelling at me while speeding up. I would always look out the window, idolizing the birds and wishing I could take flight at that moment.

Not everyone who has experienced trauma has or will experience dissociation. Some people, like myself, experienced dissociation during the traumatic event but never outside of the trauma. Some people dissociate when triggered. I've often had people who've been sexually violated tell me they dissociate during sex, even when they're having sex with their intimate partner and aren't being hurt by them. Some people dissociate when the stressful moments in life are too much to bear.

One of my workshop participants couldn't remember anything from her childhood or teenage years. Even though she can't recall anything, her healthcare providers are certain it's because she experienced significant trauma during those years, and her brain allowed her to dissociate during the traumas and the abusive situation she grew up in. Another one of my workshop participants didn't have severe dissociative symptoms like amnesia, depersonalization, and derealization from her earlier trauma until after she retired.

Just like all traumatic experiences are different, the symptoms we experience from it will be different, which also means our healing journeys will be different. We want so much for someone to give us the one solution that will work for us so we'll be magically released from our suffering. But that's not how it works. Trauma changes the structure and function of our brain. Given the significant complexity of the human brain and that each person's brain is not changed in the exact same way when exposed to trauma, there will never be a one-size-fits-all solution to trauma healing. I don't say that to discourage you. I say it so you know that the journey will be tumultuous, so you can go into the process with your eyes wide open. But life is also tumultuous. Whether you experience trauma or not, life is going to be filled with ups, downs, twists, and turns, and you're going to get bumps and bruises along the way. Resisting how life works won't change the reality of it. That's why you must find ways to weather life's storms, bandage up the wounds the storm leaves behind, and hold on to the glimmers of light whenever they show through. This book is about giving you the tools so you can do all of that. The next activity will provide you with a tool you can use when you've discovered in present moments that you've dissociated.

Activity

In this activity, you'll practice grounding. Because dissociation involves separating from the here and now, grounding helps reconnect you to the present moment. It's important to have a plan in place if you or someone else realizes you've dissociated. In the beginning, it's more likely that someone else will need to call your attention to it, until you build enough awareness to recognize when you're doing it.

You might let your family and friends know what to do if they notice you've zoned out. To capture your attention, they could call out your name, touch your arm, snap their fingers, or wave their hand in front of your face. It's also a good idea to let them know that you'll practice grounding after you snap out of it. The more people we can enlist for support in our healing journey, the safer and secure we'll feel as we progress through our painful past, and the faster we can proceed through our healing journey. Trauma healing is all about building resources and using those resources. Even though other people are often the cause of trauma, other people can also be a tremendous help in getting us through our trauma.

There are many ways to practice grounding once you become aware that you were just dissociating. For example, you could identify where you are and what you're doing at that moment, or name five things you see, hear, and feel in your present environment. I particularly like grounding techniques that can be practiced anywhere and even when you're with someone you're not comfortable with knowing what you're doing. Examples of this are pushing your feet into the ground if you're sitting and feeling where you're connected with the chair. You could also get up and move around, noticing how your feet hit the floor and the different sights, smells, and sounds around you.

Because dissociation typically happens when a person is triggered, I encourage you to try some of the intervention strategies you've already chosen, such as focusing on your breathing, reminding yourself you're safe, and vocalizing your needs if you're with another person. As I've said before, whatever coping strategy you choose when you're triggered, including when you realize you are dissociating, it's important to practice ahead of time so you'll automatically turn to the tools without needing to think about it.

Although I'm a strong proponent of finding ways for us to cope with our pain when no one else is around, I do believe it's important to seek professional help when our symptoms become too much to handle. Dissociation is a protective mechanism, so we don't have to get too close to our painful feelings at that moment. However, continually separating ourselves from our pain can slow down our progress in moving through and beyond our trauma. If not addressed, we can start using dissociation to cope with other types of stress. Over time, this could impede our success in school, our careers, and in our relationships. That's why working with a trained professional is important to work through your trauma and the symptoms you're experiencing. Again, trauma steals so much from us, so we must prevent further theft of our present and future life in any way possible.

To prevent our brain from automatically turning on the dissociative function requires us to find ways to prevent ourselves from reaching the point of extreme overwhelm when our traumatic memories revisit us. We must find ways to stay present in the moment, experience the pain, and see that we survived after the memories appeared. Once we can show our brain that we can handle the painful memories, it won't keep tapping into dissociation as a tool for coping.

Learning to let the memories come up without them overwhelming you is no easy task. That's why it's best that this initial work be done with a trained professional. Once you see that the memories can appear, but you survived even though it was hard, it'll be easier for you to do the same on your own.

How Can I Handle Anniversary Dates?

My world fell apart the moment I walked in to find the first man who made me feel like I was deserving of love and respect dead. I was 25 years old. Stan, twice my age, was an alcoholic and drug addict and on life parole — and none of that bothered me. He loved me in ways I never knew were possible. He made me feel like I deserved to have all the best this world has to offer. His sole mission in our relationship was to make me happy and do whatever he could to bring a smile to my face, even if he wasn't there to see it. I would come home to flowers on my doorstep. I would wake up in the morning to a beautiful card on my pillow. He would randomly place Hershey's Kisses around my apartment, so he could give me kisses throughout the day even when he wasn't there. He would make me the most wonderful meals. He would massage my feet and paint my toenails afterward. After he died, every holiday, birthday, special moment, painful moment, and each night that passed without him there by my side caused me to grieve.

The anniversary of his passing was always the most difficult. I would immediately go back and think about how his body looked when I found him dead on the floor. I would remember how he felt cold to the touch. I'd remember calling 911 and all aspects of the event like it was happening again. It made me dread the date because I knew what was going to happen. So, I started to plan something outside my routine for that day. I would aim to do something that would take up the entire day and be enjoyable, like going for a hike or spending time with a family member or friend. I made sure to plan the activity in advance, knowing I might have limited emotional resources for determining what to do for the anniversary.

I also stopped memorializing the date of his death. In the beginning, I would spend the anniversary looking at pictures and cards he gave me, playing songs that were significant to the both of us, and reminiscing about our best times together. This practice was not good for me in the beginning. It just kept my wound raw and didn't allow me to heal.

I'm not saying that you should never look at things that remind you of a loved one who passed, but you want to make sure you don't dig yourself even deeper if you're already in a hole. If a particular date is already triggering, and you have difficulty getting through that day, I recommend avoiding activities that make it even harder to get through that day.

In general, when you're trying to change your emotional state, aim to do something that will oppose your current emotional state. For example, if you're already down and feeling depressed, then it might not be a good idea to listen to sad, sappy songs that will bring you deeper into the unresourceful state you're already in. Instead, listen to songs that change your state. You could listen to songs that make you want to sing or dance or make you feel energized.

By doing enjoyable activities that are unrelated to your pain on the anniversary of a trauma or other significant date, you begin to replace the painful memories from that date with good memories. Over time, what was once a painful day on the calendar can become a good or neutral day. The date of Stan's passing is now a neutral day for me. I've completely divorced that date from his death, so much so that I might not remember until a few days after the date of his passing. I never thought that would be possible, but it happened because I stopped placing significance on that date, so it no longer was triggering for me. I no longer associate that date with devastation.

In the beginning, I felt a pang of sadness when I realized that I forgot about the date of his passing. I felt like I was forgetting him as I moved on with my life. But I've been able to shift my perspective and now feel immense relief that I don't remember. Not only did I used to be depressed on the day of his passing, but I would sometimes be depressed for a few days before and after. Sometimes, I couldn't function during those periods. I don't feel that being unable to live the life I still have honors the life he lost. Now I view being able to thrive in my life as the ultimate honor for the life he lost.

Now I can remember Stan on different days throughout the year without being devastated. That doesn't mean it doesn't bother me when I think about how he looked on the floor or how he felt when I touched him, but it doesn't catapult me backward into a flood of difficult emotions that I have trouble getting out of. I can be with the memory and let it go by shifting my mind to a good memory of Stan. It helps for me to look at a picture of him to focus on an image of him that's not him dead on the floor. Listening to a song that was special to us or reading a card he gave me and remembering his warm embrace helps me focus on something other than how cold his body was when I last touched him. This practice of replacing pain with something else has helped tremendously with reducing my chances of being triggered or getting stuck if I am triggered when certain dates appear on the calendar or certain memories creep into my mind.

I learned during my teenage years that I could stop associating specific dates with tragedy by distracting myself and doing something enjoyable on the anniversaries of sexual assaults and the day I was attacked from behind at knifepoint. If I had the day off school, I would plan to work on an art project — a painting, drawing, or poem — in addition to going for a long walk or riding my bike. If it was on a day I had to go to school, I would make sure it was filled with something in addition to classes, like volunteering or playing sports. I always made sure in advance that I had a full day planned so I wouldn't focus on the pain associated with that date.

Now, I can't even remember the dates of my assaults because I stopped associating specific dates on the calendar with specific traumas. Now, there is no date on the calendar that I fear because I no longer associate any date on the calendar with any of my traumas. It's hard to believe sometimes, but it's been a huge step in my healing journey. Before, I would get anxious for days before knowing the trauma anniversary was coming and that I would be flooded with terrible memories on that day. That doesn't happen now, and I no longer feel the need to plan something to do in advance on those days. They have each become just a regular day with no special significance. This doesn't mean I never get stuck thinking about my traumas; it just means that I'm not triggered by certain dates.

In the next activity, you'll have the opportunity to develop a plan to handle difficult days like the anniversary of a trauma, a birthday of a loved one you've lost, or a holiday without them there by your side. This activity is about developing strategies to decrease the likelihood that you'll be triggered on dates that are significant to you. My hope is that over time, you'll break the pattern, like I did, of associating specific dates with pain, and those days will instead become good or neutral days.

Activity

Get out your journal and identify dates on your calendar that will be difficult for you. It may be the anniversary of a trauma or the loss of a loved one. It may be a holiday, birthday, or wedding anniversary. Then brainstorm ideas for what you can do on each day that will help distract and provide you with enjoyment, so you have good emotions to counteract the difficult emotions that might still come up throughout the day.

It's important to do this ahead of time because it may be difficult to plan something on the day of if you're filled with difficult feelings and emotions.

Even with the plan you develop, you still might get triggered. If so, that is when you'll use the intervention strategies you developed. The rawer your pain, the more likely you'll be triggered. Expect that for the first few years after your trauma, you'll be triggered on dates of particular importance even if doing something enjoyable and unrelated to your trauma. That's why, when planning how to distract yourself on that day, also plan what you'll do if triggered.

As each year goes by, I'm hopeful that, like I have, you'll replace painful dates with new sensations, thoughts, and feelings so those dates no longer evoke painful thoughts and feelings.

Chapter 3

Will I Ever Heal?

Experiencing trauma is hard enough, but trying to figure out how to move past your trauma can seem impossible. It's why many people want to give up; they feel like their suffering will only end in death. It's why one of the questions I receive most is, "Will I ever heal?" Once people realize they will never be able to forget their trauma, they start to wonder if it will ever be possible to heal with painful memories forever following them around.

I can relate to every person who's asked me, "Will ever forget?" and "Will I ever heal?" because even with all I know on an intellectual level about trauma and how it affects our brain, part of me still hopes it won't affect me forever. But the truth is that we heal emotionally from trauma in a way similar to a physical wound. Over time, we may regain function but be left with a scar, a reminder of the injury. That means we must learn ways to live with a past we cannot forget. But just because we'll always remember our trauma, it doesn't mean we must suffer from it until the day we die. There is a difference between remembering our trauma and suffering from it. That's why the next chapter will focus on tools you can use to heal and minimize your suffering.

Trauma changes how we see the world. It makes us question ourselves and how we move through the world. Depending on the type, trauma can affect our ability to feel safe in the world. Because safety and security are basic human needs, trauma that makes us feel unsafe can leave us always on edge, waiting for the next danger lurking around the corner. Even though it's difficult to once again feel safe and trust oneself and others, it is possible. To move forward, you'll have to start challenging the glasses you're seeing the world through. You'll need to find ways to feel safe in the world and trust your instincts. These topics will also be covered later.

We often acquire coping mechanisms after we experience trauma that allow us to survive in the aftermath. When we practice them for long enough, these habits endure long past their usefulness. Instead of looking for evidence that your trauma is no longer affecting you, I encourage you to instead look for ways you're improving. That's the purpose of the next activity.

Activity

Get out your journal and note the ways you've improved since your trauma. If your trauma involved people you were supposed to trust, the progress you might look for is allowing yourself to be more vulnerable with people who care about you. If you're trying to rid yourself of coping mechanisms that no longer serve you, progress might be when you aren't utilizing specific coping mechanisms anymore or as often. Or, it might be when you're aware of when you are engaging in the behavior. Awareness is critical to making any change.

This activity assumes that some time has passed since your traumatic event. However, if it occurred recently, keep this activity in your back pocket, and, in the meantime, keep reminding yourself that it won't always feel as hard as it does now.

Even if a person never experiences trauma, they will always be a work in progress. There will always be times when pain from their past infiltrates their present life. There will always be habits and behaviors they could work on improving. That's why I encourage you to continue to look for evidence of how you're improving over time, but I wouldn't look for a day when your trauma never affects you again. That's an unattainable goal, and aiming for it will make you feel hopeless and helpless.

Will I Ever Be the Same?

When going through life-altering experiences, we know in our heart that we'll never be the same again. However, it's easy to cling to the possibility that we might be wrong and will be able to reclaim some semblance of the life we previously had or were reaching for before our trauma. It's why I commonly receive questions such as, "Will I ever be the same again?" Unfortunately, I must always start off with the short answer: "No."

This is where people usually get stuck after experiencing trauma. They try so hard to get back to the person and life they had before, but the reality is that trauma forever changes our lives. The same is true for people waiting for the day their trauma no longer affects them. They spend so much time and energy ruminating on the trauma, not understanding why it had to happen, and focusing on the pain and resentment they have for how their life has changed. Unfortunately, nothing can undo the trauma and the fact that our lives have been forever changed. The only thing you can do is change how you think about your trauma and move forward despite the pain you've experienced. That's why reframing, goal setting, and post-traumatic growth will each be covered in this book, so you can begin to practice control over what you can and experience something good from your trauma instead of just a lot of bad.

For right now, I think it's important to begin letting it sink in that your life was forever changed by your trauma. Wishing it wasn't that way won't change it. I don't say this to discourage you. I say it so you understand that expending energy on wishing that your trauma never happened and hoping it will never affect you again is pointless. The moment you realize this and accept it as truth, you can begin to devise a plan to move forward and work with your trauma so you can use it to your advantage. This is when doors open, so you can reach post-traumatic growth, the pinnacle of trauma healing.

Again, our mission in the meantime is to relinquish any lingering beliefs that there will come a day when the effects of our trauma will fully disappear. Trauma changes how we perceive the world around us. It's impossible for it not to change how we experience life, but it is possible to move forward after trauma occurs. From what I've experienced, we can eventually think about the trauma without it overwhelming us.

It's normal to feel angry and resentful once you realize it isn't possible to be the same person or have the same life as before. What's important is that you don't stay there and let those feelings fester for long. They're toxic. As the widely attributed quote says, "Resentment is like drinking poison and waiting for the other person to die." Any time I get locked into focusing on those who traumatized me in the past and who are hurting me today, I feel how it changes me. I cycle between anger, wanting revenge, being depressed, and feeling frustrated that they "won." These thoughts trap me. We get caught up in blaming the people who hurt us for the unresourceful state we're currently in, when in reality it's the way we're thinking about what they did to us that's trapping us. That can be a very difficult pill to swallow.

Please don't get me wrong, I do think people should shoulder blame for what they've done to us. I also think it's normal for us to feel angry and resentful for the suffering we've endured. All I'm saying is that we have no control over what happened to us, and letting our anger and resentment fester won't do anything to undo our trauma or change the people who hurt us. It will only change us. That's why we must figure out how to tell our story in a way that doesn't keep us stuck. That's the point of the reframing section in the next chapter. But for right now, it's important to understand that we suffer long after our trauma is over because of the stories we tell ourselves about our trauma. At some point, we must take charge of rewriting that story, or we will suffer until the day we die. It doesn't need to be that way. Yes, our trauma will always affect us, but it doesn't need to destroy our ability to have a life beyond our trauma.

We give our power away when we put our suffering and happiness in the hands of others. Many people will hurt us during our lives. This doesn't necessarily mean they're bad people. Most likely, they haven't figured out how to deal with their own pain, so they pass it along to others. This is why we all experience the effects of generational trauma, trauma that gets passed down from one generation to the next.

The question "Will I ever be the same?" is closely tied to the question, "How long will it take to get over it?" Some people have trouble "getting over it" because they're trying to get back to the person they were before their trauma, and that just isn't possible. Not only is it impossible to forget our trauma, but trauma changes our brain. That means the most we can do is figure out how to pick up the pieces and move forward, while trying to mend those pieces back together along the way.

Some people have trouble "getting over" their trauma because they think healing follows a concrete timeline. Sometimes the idea that we should heal in a set timeline is given to us by society. I'll never forget the time I was on the phone with a client telling me how a scary incident at work was still affecting her. Her partner heard her telling me, and I heard him yell, "That happened six months ago! Why are you still talking about it?" I've also had many clients tell me how people in their lives have commented on how they should be over what happened by now. How are they determining that timeline? Who came up with this idea that it should take a certain amount of time to get over a loss, being raped, or physically assaulted? And who exactly is determining the timeline for healing? The idea is ridiculous!

What's really going on is people want us to stop making them uncomfortable. Being with someone and their story requires empathy and compassion. In other words, it requires energy. Some people get tired of expending that energy or just don't have it in them to give. They might also not like the feelings your story brings up in them, so they want to make you stop telling it. In many ways, this is understandable. Think of how uncomfortable you've been during and after your trauma. When you're sharing your story, you transmit that discomfort to the listener, and not everyone can handle that. Most people's instinct is to push that discomfort away and resist more from coming, which is why many people will try to push you through your story and get you off topic, so they can avoid feeling any further discomfort. It's also why they'll discourage you from telling your story again and tell you that you should be over it by now. They're essentially shaming you into silence. Most people don't do this maliciously. They're just trying to protect themselves; like how we're not trying to hurt ourselves by telling ourselves we should be over it by now. We also just want to stop suffering.

It's easy to push ourselves too hard, especially when trying to get the aftermath to end as quickly as the trauma occurred. But it doesn't work like that. Some factors that affect our timeline for healing as well as the changes in our brain are the age we experienced the trauma, the type of trauma, whether there are physical reminders of the trauma (like a scar), and whether it involved another person, and whether we were supposed to be able to trust that person. It also matters what your life experiences were prior to the trauma and whether the trauma reinforced negative beliefs you already had about yourself.

This is why our healing journey requires an immense amount of self-compassion and patience with ourselves. The other thing we must be prepared for is how our trauma will always resurface from time to time, regardless of how long ago it was and how much progress we have made. I must constantly remind myself of this. I have thrived since my traumas, but there are still days when I repeat old coping mechanisms from when I was experiencing my deepest pain. Food is my best example. It is my one great love and my preferred form of self-destruction. There are still times when I am overwhelmed or depressed and overeat to self-soothe. I know it's an old habit. I know it's not good for me. But I also know it was a tool that helped me survive years of pain and gut-wrenching heartache. It's a habit, and it has served me, so it's no wonder I still turn to it when I experience pain and discomfort. In these moments when I feel like I'm backsliding, I remind myself of the progress I have made and that I'm doing the best I can to survive in the moment. I also try to focus on what I've gained from my trauma and not what I've lost and will no longer be because of it. Focusing on how far I've come, versus how far I still have to go, helps me tremendously. I think it's also important to remember that people who haven't experienced trauma are also always going to be a work in progress.

The purpose of this book is not only to give you tools to move forward after your trauma, but also to expose the beliefs you have that prevent you from moving forward. Just because people say something to us, like we should be "over it by now," doesn't mean it's true. Likewise, just because we say things to ourselves doesn't mean those things are true. We must start questioning the self-defeating messages given to us and that we give to ourselves. That's the purpose of the next activity. It will ask you to list the limiting beliefs you have about your trauma, your timeline for healing, and how you'll never be the same again. As the name implies, limiting beliefs limit us. They keep us stuck and make us feel powerless to change our circumstances. The purpose of this activity is to bring your limiting beliefs into your awareness. You can't change something unless you're first aware that it's a problem. You'll come back to these limiting beliefs in the reframing section of the next chapter, where you'll begin to challenge these beliefs. Again, for right now, you're just bringing your limiting beliefs to light. If they stay hidden in the darkness, they can continue to wreak havoc. When you bring them out into the open, you can call them out for what they are, challenge them, and release the power they have over you.

Activity

Get out your journal and write down all your limiting beliefs about your trauma, your timeline for healing, and how you'll never be the same again. If you have trouble with this activity, sit back and think about any negative thing you've thought or said related to your trauma. For your trauma, does part of you believe it was your fault or that you could have prevented it? For your healing timeline, do you think you think you should have healed sooner or should be "over it by now"? Finish the activity by writing down any limiting beliefs you have about the fact that your life will never be the same again because of your trauma. For example, do you think it sucks that you'll never be the same again, do you think you'll never be able to trust again, or do you think you'll suffer for the rest of your life?

Again, just because part of you thinks something is true, doesn't mean it is. Remember, the purpose of this activity is just to bring to your conscious mind the words you are saying to yourself that are keeping you stuck. I am hopeful that by the end of this book, you'll have new ways of thinking and new ways to handle negative thoughts and behaviors that prevent you from moving forward into the life you desire and deserve.

I've been asked by people who feel that they've healed from their trauma, "Why didn't I heal sooner?" We heal in the time frame we're able to. There is so much that needs to be done to move forward, and moving forward in one aspect of our lives often requires first moving forward in a different aspect of our lives. For example, in my life, I believe it was important to acknowledge all the times I was violated as a child and teenager. However, I couldn't acknowledge all the people who had hurt me until I had healthy coping mechanisms in place to deal with the flood of emotions that would come with unpacking all the secrets I had been carrying. Trauma overwhelms our capacity to cope, so we latch on to anything that gives us a moment's relief from our suffering and memories. I latched on to food, alcohol, and sex with strangers to cope. None of these were, of course, healthy, but they allowed me to survive long enough to figure out how to move forward. I had to first figure out how to replace these unhealthy coping strategies with healthy ones, so I didn't resume old behaviors once I started to address the secrets from my past. Although I wish I could have made progress faster in my healing journey, I don't think it was possible for me to go faster than I did. I moved at exactly the pace I needed to go so I could progress through the necessary steps to move forward. I believe the same will be true for you.

Will I Ever Be Happy Again?

Trauma can be soul-crushing. It feels like our life was stolen from us, and in many ways it has been. It's difficult to even imagine that you could ever be happy after your world fell to pieces. When I tell you that you'll never be able to forget your trauma and never be the same again, it could be easy to think you'll never pick up your broken pieces. But that's not the purpose of me sharing those messages. It's so you stop holding on to unattainable goals. Reaching for something you'll never be able to grasp will only leave you feeling more hopeless. What is an attainable goal, however, is to be happy again. I know in the immediate aftermath of trauma, being happy again seems impossible. But it is. Even though I've experienced a significant amount of devastation in my life, I've also experienced a significant amount of beauty, joy, love, and happiness.

I don't usually have difficulty answering questions that my clients ask me about healing from trauma, because I've had the same questions and spent my life figuring out the answers for myself. But there was one question that made me pause and say I would get back to her with an answer. She mentioned how I'm happy most of the time and asked how she could do the same. More specifically, she wanted to know how to find joy in little things, and in people and processes she doesn't particularly like. I went to open my mouth with an answer, and nothing came out, which surprised me, as I'm not usually at a loss for words. I know I am happy and bubbly most of the time, but I've never thought about how I got to be this way. That's why I had to spend time reflecting on why I'm so joyous, how I'm able to find joy in the smallest things, and being this way since I was young when I was experiencing numerous forms of trauma.

What I determined is that feeling joy is a choice I've made. I never wanted my abusers and the numerous disgusting people in this world to steal my joy from me. I considered practicing joy and being happy when others tried to steal it from me as an act of defiance, and it made me feel like I was winning the battle. Some of my abusers were trying to break me and steal my smile. They would tell me I was so stupid, disgusting, and that I was nothing. Still smiling, being happy, and going on about my life as though what they did and said to me didn't affect me was my way of standing up to them and saying that I refuse to let them destroy me. Focusing on being happy and the things that made me smile also meant I wasn't focusing on my pain, which made me want to do it more. Eventually, finding joy became a habit and didn't require much thought, but like any habit, if not practiced for a period, it can break.

In my mid-twenties, I experienced a particularly severe bout of depression. I can easily say that happened not just because of the circumstances in my life, but because of what I was focusing on. I stopped focusing on the beauty in every moment, and when that happened, I could only see the devastation surrounding me. It wasn't until I changed what I was focusing on that I was able to get out of my rut. That involved practicing gratitude and finding joy in every moment again. It still happens to me today. I can tell that whenever I experience a bout of depression, overwhelm, or any other undesirable feeling, it's because I haven't been focusing on the "right" things, like what I have to be grateful for and something beautiful in every moment.

All we ever have is this one moment. Paying attention to each moment as if it were our last can completely transform the way we experience life. The purpose of the next activity is to encourage you to begin practicing gratitude in random moments throughout the day so you can see there is always some glimmer of hope to hold on to in your moments of darkness.

Activity

To begin practicing gratitude randomly throughout the day, start right now. What is one thing you are grateful for at this moment? Is it that the sun is shining, is it a loved one, this book, or that you woke up today?

To continue with this practice, set an alarm to go off at different intervals throughout the day to remind you to find something you're grateful for at that moment, regardless of where you are or what you're doing. Use your phone, watch, or bedside clock to set an alarm for every two hours after you wake up. When the alarm goes off, find one thing at that moment you're grateful for. I encourage you to practice this for at least a few days, but preferably for a week so you can practice finding something to be grateful for at any point during the day. The point of this exercise is for you to see that there is always something positive you can hold on to. This is important when we reach low points in our lives. These moments of gratitude give us hope, which can help us make it through life's inevitable challenges.

I also encourage you to find at least one thing you're grateful for each time you wake up from a night's sleep or a nap. Sleeping is like hitting a reset button, so even if you fall asleep after a hard day or after something difficult happened, it's like a new beginning when you wake up. That's why it's important to start each new beginning strongly. Beginning it with something positive like pointing out at least one thing you're grateful for is a good way to start. Likewise, it's important to start your sleep right by thinking about at least one thing you're grateful for before you fall asleep.

I realize that some days might be challenging to find anything to be grateful for, but still find at least one thing. It'll be most important on those hard days. In a workshop I participated in, one person said that on their hard days they always say, "I'm grateful I'm not on fire." She said that some days that's the best she can do, but at least she can always be grateful for something when life is difficult. What will be your go-to for practicing gratitude when it seems like life can't get any worse?

When you're doing this exercise, notice whether you're resisting the practice of finding something good in random moments of the day. Are you saying things like "This is dumb" or "This isn't going to make any difference"? It's important to become aware of such resistance, because these types of language patterns will keep you stuck. You'll never be able to love life again if you only focus on pain. It just isn't possible. To experience life in a different way, you must think and act differently. If you only focus on the pain in your life, you'll begin to think life is all about suffering. But once you see that life can be beautiful, you begin to challenge the belief that you'll never be happy again.

It sucks that we've had to endure the traumas we have, and it sucks that we must figure out a way to move on after they occur, but we must figure out a way just the same. We may not have deserved what happened to us, but we do deserve the opportunity to live and be happy again. Yes, trauma steals our joy for a period, but it doesn't need to steal it forever.

It's so easy to collect evidence of how our life has been marred by our trauma; that's why it can take a lot of effort to find bits of our life that are still good or at least getting better after experiencing trauma. But it's an important practice. We must practice gratitude when we don't feel like it, so we have a tool to be able to get us out of the darkness our trauma traps us in. As you collect things you're grateful for, it'll be easier to smile, and the load you're carrying will feel a little lighter. Eventually, your trauma won't become the focal point of your life, but just one part of your story. Then you'll see how to become the narrator of your story and choose the direction your life will go, versus having your trauma dictate the direction of your life. This has happened in my life.

With trauma covering the majority of my life, I never thought my suffering would end and life would get better, but they have. Yes, I'll always be triggered and remember my traumas from time to time, and, yes, I may also experience PTSD and depression symptoms from time to time, but they no longer consume my life. I've chosen to fill my life with as much hope, joy, and laughter as possible. My traumas have stolen so much from me; they don't deserve more. It's within my power to determine how much more of my life I'll give away to my traumas. Each time I choose to look for beauty in the darkness and smile instead of cry, I'm declaring to my traumas, "No more! You're not getting one more piece of me." You can choose to do the same.

You don't need beautiful views, sunshine, or to be feeling good to experience joy. Feeling joy is a choice. In every moment, whether that moment is good or bad, we have the choice to be happy. I hope you can find something beautiful in your day today, and every day.

Chapter 4

How Do I Heal?

When people get to the point that they believe it's possible to heal after their trauma, their next question becomes, "How do I do it?" It can seem overwhelming to figure out how to pick up your broken pieces after the devastation you've experienced, but deciding you're ready and willing to do that work is the most important step you'll take in your healing journey.

I'm often asked during podcast interviews and by the loved ones of individuals who have experienced trauma how to help people who've experienced trauma get through it. The first thing I tell them is that the person must be ready to change. People often look at me, shocked, after I say this, because they can't imagine that someone who has been self-destructing and feeling depressed wouldn't want to change. However, I know from experience that when you're in a deep hole, it seems impossible that there could ever be a way out. When that hopelessness sets in, you feel there's no point in trying.

There are also some people who don't want to give up the attention they get from being "damaged." This is particularly true of people who have felt insignificant for most of their lives. When they go from being starved of attention before their trauma to being showered with attention afterward, it's hard to give that attention up. Even if the attention comes in the form of criticism and condemnation for the way they're self-destructing, at least they're finally being seen. I know the feeling of being invisible well. I combatted my feelings of being invisible and insignificant by showing my bubbly personality and big smile and striving for big goals that would make people notice. Others combat their feelings of insignificance by staying in victim mode. Every thought, behavior, and habit we have, we have because it's served us in some way. People trapped in despair sometimes stay there because the reward for staying there appears greater than the reward for getting out.

Sometimes the benefits of staying trapped come in the form of being able to engage in coping strategies that have negative consequences, because they like the feeling that comes with using those strategies. Drinking, using drugs, and having sex with random strangers, for example, can feel good in the moment. If they were to get healthy, they would have to give those strategies up and the feelings that come with them.

That's why it's such a big deal when you decide that enough is enough, that you're tired of living the way you are, and you're ready to figure a way out. But it can take a lot of time and a lot more suffering to get there. I had to fall pretty far after Stan died to decide I wanted to live and stop hurting myself. The journey since that decision has been long, bumpy, and I've stumbled and gotten off course many times, but, ultimately, I keep moving forward. Each time I get off track, I turn to the steps I've used to get back on track in the past, so I can get back to my journey forward. That's the purpose of this chapter, to give you the three steps I turn to each time I'm off course: goal setting, reframing, and self-care.

Goal setting allows me to envision a future that separates me from my unchangeable past and present pain. At my lowest point, I had to start out with the basics, like cleaning my body and home because I didn't feel worthy of even that. But as I started taking these smaller steps, it got easier to do the next. Reframing is about changing your perspective. When at that low point, I started to focus on what I gained from my trauma, instead of on all I had lost and that would no longer be because of my trauma. I focused on how strong I must be to have survived. I focused on my deep sense of empathy and compassion for those in pain because of my deep knowledge of pain. Self-care was again hard for me because I didn't feel worthy, but it was a critical step. Trauma overwhelms our capacity to cope, so to progress through it, we must find ways to cope that don't harm us. The coming sections will cover each step in greater detail.

I liked what psychiatrist Dr. Bruce Perry said about therapy in the book, *What Happened to You?* He said, "It is almost as if therapy is taking your two-lane dirt road and building a four-lane freeway alongside it. The old road stays, but you don't use it much anymore. Therapy is building a better alternative, a new default."[5] I highly recommend you go to therapy to help work through your trauma, but there are things you'll have to do outside of therapy to make progress. I've been in therapy for many years, but my therapist can't be with me every day to do the actual work of moving forward and figuring out how to handle the stress of living on top of my traumatic stress. I need to do that work on my own.

This book is about giving you tools for when you're on your own. It's important to have other people to lean on when we're healing from trauma, but the person we need to be able to count on most is oneself. It's empowering when you know you can shoulder the hard days on your own, knowing you have the tools in place to handle anything that gets in your way on your path to healing.

Dr. Perry's analogy using the dirt road and freeway resonated with me in many ways. When I'm literally and figuratively traveling a dirt road, I must move slower, and the ride is bumpier and because of that more painful. Whereas when I'm traveling on a literal or figurative highway, I'm able to travel more quickly and have a smoother and less painful ride. The more I heal, the less likely I am to be diverted back onto the dirt road when I'm triggered to remember my traumas or when life stressors mount. When I'm regularly using my tools to work through past and present stress, I'm able to stay on the highway. Because I'm still on the highway, I can move through painful memories more quickly, and I'm less likely to be derailed by the memories. I'm also able to be more resilient with new stressors and less likely to be sidelined by them. My hope is that this book will give you the tools to do the same. The more tools we can add to our toolbox, the more resourceful we'll be under times of stress.

Self-Care

Although I experienced numerous traumas starting from a young age, I never talked about any of them until I was 25. I knew that ignoring my traumas wasn't working, but I also knew I couldn't bear all the memories that I had locked away in the deepest recesses of my mind all rushing out at the same time. It was at 25 that I chose to find my first therapist. I first met with the therapist right before Stan and I were about to close on the house we would be moving into. Even though I had just started the first semester of my PhD program, I was ready to discuss my traumas so I could move beyond them. Unfortunately, life had more traumas in store for me.

The same day I decided to tell Stan about the traumas I was starting to address, his mom was diagnosed with terminal cancer. His mom meant so much to him, so how could I now burden him with my past? I couldn't. So, to continue the trend of keeping my secrets to myself, I decided to wait to tell him. A few weeks after her diagnosis, she died with Stan and I by her side. It was the first time I had ever watched someone die, and I started a new job a few hours after she passed away. As per usual, I had to go into my new job pretending life was great when it was anything but.

Stan started to fall apart after his mother died. His drinking and drug use went up. I knew I couldn't burden him with my pain, but I was dying inside. I was reliving traumas I had kept buried deeply for years. I had waited to talk about them until I had someone to lean on, and that person was crumbling. I thought things couldn't get any worse, until I walked in to find Stan dead two weeks after his mom died. I closed on the house we were supposed to move into a week and a half later, on the same day my first semester of my PhD program finished. On top of all this, I had to pack up all my stuff at my apartment and move into my new home.

The move helped keep my breakdown at bay for a little while because it gave me something else to focus on. My family was great at helping me with my move and fixing up things in the house that Stan was supposed to do when we first moved in. But after the dust settled, I was left in the house by myself, and every time I looked around, I was forced to think about the plans Stan and I made for each room. The silence in my new home was the perfect place for the traumas I was reliving to come out and play. In between thinking about the plans Stan and I had for the house and what it was like to see and feel his cold body on the floor, I was having flashbacks of the many rapes and other forms of abuse I had experienced during my life.

I stayed in the new job for as long as I could but eventually became incapable of working. However, never having a reason to regularly leave my home once I stopped working was not good for me. My depression became severe, and I contemplated suicide daily. I wasn't bathing, brushing my teeth, or cleaning my home because I didn't feel worthy of even the most basic forms of self-care. My external environment became a true reflection of what was going on inside me. It mirrored the deep sense of disgust I felt about myself. When I did leave my home, it was to go to a bar to seek out random men that reminded me of Stan. I was also putting on weight at a rapid pace, which caused stretch marks to sprout across my stomach as visible evidence and permanent reminders of my suffering.

My mother did the best she could to help me financially while I couldn't work, but I still ended up with tax liens on my home and calls from debt collectors. I had considered prostituting myself for income. I figured since I was already sleeping with so many strange men, I might as well get compensated for it. I went so far as to post ads on Craigslist to advertise that I was willing to exchange sexual favors for financial rewards. To this day, I am extremely grateful that each ad got flagged for removal and I never went down that path, but it still hurts that I would have.

After months of helping me and seeing that I was just getting worse, my mother gave me an ultimatum: "Either get help, or I'm going to stop helping you financially." Even though it hurt, the best thing she could have done for me was to stop helping me. It forced me to make a choice: did I want to keep going down the path I was on, or did I want to figure a way out? I wanted to figure a way out.

When my mom delivered her ultimatum, she came with a therapist's name and number in hand. My, sister, Christina is a therapist, and she found a therapist who was highly recommended. This was important because I had stopped seeing the one I first started with after only a few months when she told me I would never heal unless I accepted God into my life. Feeling abandoned by God since childhood, this crushed me. It further traumatized me even though she was supposed to be helping me work through my traumas.

It took time to get in to see my new therapist. I also knew that once I started seeing a therapist, they wouldn't be able to be with me every minute of the day. I needed to figure out a way to get through hard days, in times no one else was around. I also wanted to make changes as soon as I decided I wanted to live. I knew I had to take advantage of that crucial decision and start building momentum right away.

I knew I needed to start working again but couldn't go straight into looking for a job. I first needed to work on bathing and leaving my home. To do this, I wrote down goals for myself each day.

There will be a whole section on goal setting in this chapter because of how important it has been in my healing journey, but for now, it's important to know that the first goals I set for myself were self-care, like brushing my teeth, bathing, and taking out the trash. I had to force myself to practice the most basic forms of self-care, self-compassion, and self-love, even though I didn't feel worthy. People often think they must wait to practice self-care and other forms of self-love until they feel deserving, but the reality is that you need to force yourself to do the self-care practices, so you'll begin to feel worthy. I realize this is easier said than done. I couldn't start forcing myself to practice self-care until I decided that part of me wanted to live.

As these initial goals became habits, I no longer needed to keep writing them down and could instead write down other goals, like applying for a certain number of jobs each day. However, my initial self-care goals were some of the hardest because I didn't feel deserving, but as I cleaned my body and home, I started to feel better, which made it easier to take other steps to change how I was experiencing life. Eventually, I felt strong and confident enough to start working again. Once I began working, my pride and confidence grew further, and all aspects of my life began to improve. It all began with self-care.

Activity

Decide which one or two self-care practices you can incorporate into your daily routine today. The self-care practices you use will vary based on where you are in your healing journey. Meet yourself where you're currently at. If you aren't practicing basic self-care like bathing, brushing your teeth, or cleaning your home, then start there. If you're doing basic self-care practices, then proceed with additional steps that will help build a sense of self-love, compassion, and possibly even pride in yourself. I encourage you to do this by working on the things you say to yourself each day. This could involve acknowledging your positive attributes, celebrating your wins, or stopping yourself from talking negatively about yourself.

As you get stronger, I encourage you to expand on practices that improve your health, such as exercise, food and liquids that nurture your body, proper amounts of sleep, and minimizing your time around toxic people. As you take care of all aspects of your physical and emotional health, the benefits will seep into all aspects of your life. As they do, they will begin to combat the tentacles your trauma has used to steal life from you.

It's important to keep in mind that a tool that worked at one stage of your healing journey may not be as useful in another stage, so be willing to continually adapt and learn new ways to heal. Also keep in mind that life is cyclical, so you might need to revert to your initial forms of self-care many years down the road when life throws another roadblock in your way. The point of this book is for you to begin adding tools to your toolbox so you can chip away at the chains that keep you anchored to your traumatic past, nurse your wounds, and build yourself back up stronger than before so you can handle the inevitable hardship life will continue to bring to your door.

Self-care isn't about spending money. Many people think self-care is about getting a massage or your hair or nails done. Although self-care can involve spending money on yourself at regular intervals, it's about the way you show up for yourself each day in the ways you need. Self-care not only involves tending to your basic needs for survival and providing yourself with ways to cope with difficult circumstances, but self-care is also about rejuvenation and enriching your life.

If you need additional self-care ideas, my book, *Transformation After Trauma: Embracing Post-Traumatic Growth*, details a variety of self-care tools along with instructions on how to incorporate each tool into your life. However, don't overwhelm yourself by doing too many things at once. If you're not bathing, brushing your teeth, or cleaning your home, consider starting with just one of those activities. Once it becomes a habit or you begin feeling better, you'll be able to do more without getting overwhelmed. I know it can be frustrating to think how long it might take to get out of your suffering if you move slowly, but slow movement forward is better than no movement at all. Keep in mind that the small, incremental changes you start with will compound over time. Between this compound effect and the momentum you'll build by taking consistent action over time, you'll end up with big shifts in less time than you think. Just because you move slowly in the beginning, doesn't mean you'll keep moving slowly.

It's normal to not feel like doing this work, especially in the beginning of your healing journey when you may not feel deserving or aren't sure whether you want to keep fighting to survive. In the beginning, any step forward is going to feel hard, very hard. This difficulty is going to make you question whether you want to do the work and whether the effort will pay off. But you must force yourself to do the work even though you don't feel like it and aren't sure whether it will even matter. You must push through any resistance you face from the stories in your mind. You must put up this fight, or your past will keep stealing life from you.

I understand that you might be resentful about having to do this work and keep fighting for your survival because of something someone did to you or circumstances that were out of your control. However, resisting the work won't change the fact that it needs to be done. No one else can do this work for us. Even if someone else caused us to suffer, we're the only ones who determine whether we'll continue to suffer from our trauma. Just because we'll never be able to forget our trauma doesn't mean we must spend the rest of our life suffering.

We can't control the fact that our trauma occurred, and we can't control what we've done to survive that we may regret. The only thing we have control over is how we think about our trauma and what we do moving forward from this moment on. It's empowering when we begin to learn how to practice control in healthy ways after we lost control during our trauma.

Self-care is about engaging in activities to take care of our emotional, mental, and physical health. Positive self-care practices can improve our mood, reduce anxiety and depression, and improve our relationship with ourselves and others. I emphasize "positive" self-care because over time we can develop "negative" self-care habits. For example, when we experience extremes of thoughts, feelings, or emotions, we might overeat, drink, use drugs, oversleep, or spend hours watching TV or on social media, even when we have a lot to do. Using negative self-care habits as coping mechanisms can cause a host of issues, depending on what your preferred maladaptive coping mechanisms are.

It makes sense why we turn to unhealthy coping strategies. As I've said before, trauma overwhelms our capacity to cope, so we hold on to anything that gives us a moment's relief from our suffering. It's easy to turn to food, drugs, alcohol, or sex to cope with the pain because these quickly release feel-good chemicals in our brain. After experiencing trauma, it makes sense that we turn to something that gives us a break from our suffering, even if for a moment. The problem is that, over time, pushing away our emotions and painful memories becomes a habit, and the strategies we use to numb our pain also prevent us from fully experiencing the beauty in life. This keeps us trapped in the belief that we'll forever suffer after we experience trauma.

People are so scared of remembering their trauma, but the reality is that they've already faced the worst of it. Yes, it's difficult to predict when the memories will make an appearance and for how long they will stay, but the reality is that they are only memories. Trying to avoid experiencing the memories or the full extent of them can make us dependent on unhealthy coping strategies that trap us deeper and longer in our suffering. That's why I asked you in Chapter 2 to develop a plan to handle the moments you're triggered, but that plan you created was reactionary.

Yes, it's important to handle the moments of extreme overwhelm. However, if you don't have a plan in place to prevent yourself from becoming overwhelmed, you'll always be putting out one fire after another, versus minimizing the chances a fire will occur in the first place. That's the focus of this chapter. When you're practicing positive self-care daily, you'll be less likely to need your action plan from Chapter 2 because you'll be less likely to be overwhelmed by previous triggers. I know this is true from my own experience.

I understand it's not easy to face everything right away, which is why you may need to do it in stages. Patricia, the therapist I found after my mother threatened to cut off my financial support unless I got help, has helped tremendously in my healing. Patricia and I took a break from working together for a few years when she moved away. When she came back, I told her that my experiences with other therapists after her didn't go so well. I told her how much I appreciated her being a partner on my journey and never pushing me farther and faster than I was ready for.

During our first session back together, I told her about all the discoveries I had made about my traumas since I last saw her. I told her that, as I went through my old journals and poems for content for my first book, I figured out which and how many men had violated me. I told her that I didn't know until I sifted through those pages of memories that eight men had sexually violated me between the ages of 9 and 19, and three were family members. That didn't even count the time I was attacked from behind at knifepoint and the numerous men who had grabbed my breasts and buttocks and tried to kiss me without my permission. As I was walking toward the door after our first session back together, Patricia mentioned how I thanked her for not pushing me faster or farther than I was ready for, but then I told her about all these abuses she never knew about. She said she wondered if she should've pushed me to get more of my past out.

I said to her, "Back then, how could I have handled acknowledging that eight men had sexually violated me and three were family members? I was barely surviving and was contemplating suicide when I came to you. I couldn't have handled more. I needed to build up more resources to be ready to process additional memories."

Most of my other therapists didn't work out because they wanted to force me to move faster than I was ready to go. Yes, I do believe that we need to process what we've been through to move beyond it, but I also believe we need to be ready to handle the onslaught of emotions and memories that come with addressing traumas or components of our traumas we've locked away deep inside. The moment I counted out the men who had hurt me, gave each a name when possible, and then put them on a timeline, I began sobbing. I even needed to take a break from working on my first book for a few months because it felt like I had been punched in the gut when I put all my traumas together for the first time. But I was able to get through it because, at that time in my life, I was dedicating a significant portion of each day to positive self-care. I was regularly walking, hiking, doing yoga, meditating, spending time with people who loved and cared about me, and taking time to sit with my thoughts to work through them.

Once I could handle owning my story and the memories that came with it, I reached a new level in my healing journey. I couldn't have done a bit of it without the internal and external resources that practicing regular positive self-care gave me. Because I had so many positive self-care strategies to choose from, I didn't revert to old unhealthy coping strategies that would have just made my onslaught of memories worse.

There are many ways to practice positive self-care. It can involve eating a healthy diet or getting plenty of sleep and exercise. It can include meditation, going for walks, spending time with people you enjoy being around, or looking for opportunities to laugh. The most wonderful thing of all is that by working toward incorporating more positive self-care into your life and beginning to replace negative self-care habits, you'll start to see improvements in many areas, if not all areas, of your life.

The first section of this chapter is dedicated to self-care because it is one of the most important things you can do to handle any type of stress, including traumatic stress. However, it takes consistent practice to make it part of your lifestyle. You need to view it as an essential part of your life. It'll be difficult to see the benefits of it if you only practice self-care occasionally. It's like exercise; you don't truly see the benefits unless you exercise regularly.

Taking care of your own needs if, and only if, you have time is a sure-fire way to never have your own needs met. Our lives are so filled with obligations and distractions that if we don't make a point to practice self-care every day, it'll likely never happen. Or it'll happen so infrequently that it won't make much difference. That's why you must put yourself first each day.

Most people don't put themselves first because of time concerns, but they don't understand how much more efficient they will be in every area of life once they feel better. When you dedicate time each day to taking care of yourself, you'll be in a better mood and feel better. When you feel good and your spirits are high, it'll improve how you interact with those around you and, therefore, improve your relationships. When you feel good, you'll be better able to focus, which will improve your productivity at work and with your obligations at home. When you feel good, you're more likely to exercise, to make better dietary choices, and are less likely to engage in unhealthy habits like drinking and smoking. Just like trauma and other forms of stress can negatively impact all areas of our life, positive self-care can positively impact all areas of our life, but this kind of positive change takes time and consistent effort.

This is where people often misstep. Just because negativity can quickly impact all areas of life, doesn't mean positivity works the same way. We live in a negative world. We are surrounded by negativity at every turn from the news, social media, the people we surround ourselves with, and the voices inside our own heads. That's why it's easy for negativity to grab hold and taint every area of our life so quickly. We're exposed to positivity much less frequently because humans have a negativity bias. We pay more attention to negative information than positive because negative input is important to pay attention to for our survival. We must know when we're in danger, so our brains are wired to look for things that could harm us. Because most positive information isn't essential to our basic survival, our brain doesn't hold on to it the same way it does negative information. Because our world is filled with so much stress and misery, it takes constant effort to overlook the pain and gravitate toward the positive. That's why positive self-care must be a daily practice for it to be effective. It doesn't need to take a long time or be the same activities each day; it just needs to be a certain amount of time each day dedicated purely to taking care of yourself.

As the common saying goes, "You can't pour from an empty cup." If you don't make sure to refill your cup every day, your cup will soon be empty, and you won't have anything else to give to anyone, including yourself. This is when extreme overwhelm hits us, when we feel that we have no more to give. By making self-care a daily practice, you'll have the resources available to handle past trauma and prevent moments of extreme overwhelm in the future.

How Can I Work Through Thoughts of Being Disgusting?

The belief that I'm disgusting runs deep in me, and it's been difficult to excavate. This isn't surprising given the significant number of sexual violations I've experienced, and how some men degraded me beyond the sexual violation itself. An example that is always clear in my mind are the times, when I was twelve, one of my abusers would grab the fat on my stomach and say, "Look at you. You're so disgusting. You should be grateful that I even want to touch you."

It's not surprising that my stomach is the area of my body I'm most critical of and I point to as "evidence" that I am disgusting. The significant changes in weight I've experienced made it worse. After Stan died, my weight jumped from 150 pounds to over 200. I developed red stretch marks and rolls of fat, which made me further despise my stomach. I'm now 138 pounds. I had hoped to start feeling less disgust when looking at my stomach after I reached a normal weight, but that didn't happen. Now, I just focus on the extra skin, cellulite, and silver stretch marks. This is why I've developed the practice of wrapping my arms around my stomach, like I'm giving myself a hug, and saying, "Thank you, body." I now look for any opportunity I can to thank my body for the amazing work it does, from my heart beating and my lungs bringing in more life with each breath, to my digestive tract when it cleanses my body of waste.

Sometimes when I thank my body, I wrap one arm around my stomach and place the other on my chest so I can feel my heartbeat. I'm always filled with immense gratitude when I focus on the fact that my heart is still beating after so many years of contemplating ending my life and putting myself in situations where that was more likely to happen. In many ways, I shouldn't still be here, and it's a miracle I'm alive, so still having a heartbeat is an easy thing to thank my body for. To combat the disgust I have for areas of my body, like my stomach, it has helped me to focus on the areas of my body that fill me with fascination and awe over how it works.

Feeling disgusting or dirty is common with certain types of traumas, particularly sexual trauma. However, these thoughts can also come with physical and emotional traumas. These thoughts can lead to self-loathing and various forms of self-harm, both of which I'm well acquainted with. Mine included a severe eating disorder and having sex with more men than I dare to count, all in an effort to try to prove to myself that I wasn't disgusting and was lovable. I will discuss this further when I address how to stop promiscuity in a later chapter, but I had convinced myself that if a man wanted to touch me, that meant that I was worthy of being touched and my body wasn't disgusting.

The only way I've been able to work through this feeling of being dirty and disgusting has been to prove to myself otherwise through self-care practices. A specific self-care practice I've found beneficial in working through my feelings of being disgusting is massaging myself with lotion. It lets me give attention to all different aspects of my body and work on showing each part of my body love instead of contempt. You'll have the opportunity to practice this yourself in the next activity.

Activity

Taking the time to focus on showing your body love and compassion through positive self-touch is a particularly powerful practice if you engage in behaviors that harm your body. This is your opportunity to thank your body for all it's capable of doing and apologize to your body and to yourself for the ways you've been unkind to yourself. This is not meant to be for you to ruminate over the ways you've harmed your body, but for you to recognize that you have hurt yourself and are working on doing better through the practice of self-massage using lotion.

Even though it may feel uncomfortable touching your body, still carefully put lotion everywhere, so you can remind yourself over and over that your body deserves and yearns to be touched in a positive way. Start with either your fingers or toes and focus on what it feels like to touch your body in this way. In the beginning, it may be helpful to look at your body with curiosity as you get to know it in this new way. It may be helpful to slowly wiggle your fingers and toes, watch how they move, and think of how amazing it is to be a human; think of everywhere our feet can take us and everything our intricate hands allow us to do that other living beings cannot. Begin to cultivate a sense of fascination, wonder, and appreciation for your body and all it can do. During the massage and throughout each day, I encourage you to thank your body for all it does.

Once you do your fingers, progress in the same fashion toward your shoulders. Likewise, once you do your toes, progress toward your hips. In the beginning, massage to where you can go without being triggered. If you've been sexually violated, it may be difficult for you to focus on massaging your breasts or buttocks in the beginning. Or if you have visible scars from your trauma, it may be difficult to touch that area. You may have areas that you're particularly critical of that you point to as "evidence" that you're disgusting. If you're having trouble concentrating on a specific area, then do that area quickly or skip it. Meet yourself where you're currently at. Over time, you'll be able to touch yourself in these places to show that you can be touched there without being hurt, but it may take time to get to that point. In the meantime, work on getting closer and closer to that area with each massage. Once you do massage an area previously avoided, you can work up to massaging it for longer periods. This is your opportunity to see that the touch you're experiencing right now is completely within your control. It's a way to reclaim control over your body.

I encourage you to make self-massage a regular practice. You can make it part of your morning or nighttime routine, or do it each time you get out of the shower.

Eventually, you can progress further to having someone else massage you so you can train your brain that it's okay for you to be touched in this way and that you deserve to be touched in a way that doesn't harm you. You may want to start with your partner or with a family member or friend by having them massage your hands and forearms or feet and lower legs. Then you can consider getting a professional massage. You could begin with a manicure that includes a hand massage or a pedicure that includes a foot massage. Then you could progress to a full body massage. It will be an enormous relief when you can see that your body isn't too disgusting to touch and healing to know that another person can touch your body without hurting you.

If at any point you're triggered during a self-massage or a massage by another person, remember the intervention strategies you developed in Chapter 2. If during a massage you begin criticizing yourself, then acknowledge the harmful self-talk, apologize to yourself, and tell yourself you are deserving of compassion, kind words, and gentle touch. You want to do better by your mind and body than others have, or you have done in the past. Be mindful to not compound your trauma by victimizing yourself with hurtful words and actions. Whenever you catch yourself doing either, recommit to caring for your mind and body in the ways you've been yearning for.

Even with a plan to fight feelings of self-loathing and feeling disgusting, please be prepared for these feelings to never fully go away. It depends how deeply rooted these beliefs are. Mine are deeply rooted beliefs whose seeds were planted in me at a young age, so I might never be able to pull up every root. This means there will always be times when these thoughts and feelings creep into my mind and that they'll likely be at their worst when I'm already feeling down. Unfortunately, negative beliefs like to come out and play when we're at emotional low points. They're like a virus. Viruses can stay hidden in our body and only activate when our body's defenses are low. Negative beliefs are like viruses of the mind. They are there, just waiting for the perfect time to attack.

They know our resistance to them will be low when we're already combating feelings of not being good enough.

This means it'll take constant practice to fight the negative beliefs we have about ourselves. Whether those beliefs are that we're disgusting, unlovable, or not good enough, it'll take constant effort to keep these inner demons at bay. That's why you need multiple tools to stay in the fight and why this book is about arming you with those tools. It might be disheartening to think that you'll always be battling your inner demons. However, I encourage you to think about how this battle will make you stronger. The strength and knowledge gained along the way will lead you into post-traumatic growth and becoming the person you never could have been without your trauma.

This is why hiking has been so important in my healing journey. It's given me a way to see how strong I am mentally and physically and to see how I grow stronger from one hike to the next. It's helped me to feel immense gratitude for my body and has helped me combat my feelings of disgust. But again, those feelings are still there. I'm just constantly doing what I can to cut them back. Like hardy weeds, negative beliefs don't require much to grow and flourish, so you must keep pulling them up each time they grow back.

You may not choose to do the self-massage or a form of physical activity, but I encourage you to find some way to regularly practice gratitude for your body so you can combat negative beliefs you have about it. I also encourage you to develop a practice of what you're going to do each time you catch yourself saying or thinking something negative about your body or looking at it in a negative way. I choose to say I'm sorry to my body and follow it with a thank-you for all it does for me, but what works for me may not work for you. Try out a few different things and see what works for you so you can stop your negative self-talk and replace it with language that better serves you.

Just because others have treated us harshly, doesn't mean we should do the same to ourselves. We should do the exact opposite. Even without experiencing trauma, it's easy to criticize our bodies with the barrage of media messages telling us all the ways we're not good enough so we'll buy their products. Put the messaging from society on top of the messaging from our abusers and from ourselves, and it creates the perfect breeding ground for self-loathing. We must do whatever we can to counteract the attacks on us from both external and internal sources. Even if you have had a self-destructive narrative on replay in your mind for many years, it's within your power to change that narrative. Yes, your mind will keep wanting to turn to the old story, but it's within your power to bring your mind back to a new, more empowering narrative.

Goal Setting

Goals give us a new way to define ourselves. I've always refused to allow my traumas to define me. It's why I've always pushed myself to reach big goals like earning my PhD, traveling around the world, being a professor, writing books, and climbing tall mountains. Instead of calling myself a victim, I called myself by all the things I am now or would be in the future.

When I tell people I don't like to define myself as a survivor, they ask what I want to be called instead. I always say, "How about a writer, world traveler, professor, or mountaineer?" I refuse to be defined by something someone else did to me and circumstances that were out of my control. I choose to be defined by what is within my control and what I have chosen to become. Defining myself based on my traumas limits me. Even though I have survived sexual trauma, I resist being identified as a survivor and using that term to describe myself, because the more it is used to describe me, the more it's ingrained in my mind that I will forever be marked and chained to my past by something someone else did to me. That thought is depressing and makes me feel unresourceful. But it's empowering to think of what I have done and will do with my life even though people and circumstances have tried to keep me down. That's why goal setting has always been so important to me; it allows me to move away from a past I cannot change and toward a future that is within my control. That's empowering; whereas, focusing on something painful and out of my control that happened to me is disempowering, and I refuse to continually focus on it. Having goals gives us something other than our pain and unchangeable past to focus on. This allows us to have hope, which is critical because trauma can make us lose hope for our future ever being better than our present or past.

Even though I like to aim for big goals to further separate myself from my unchangeable past, it doesn't mean all my goals have been big or that you need to set big goals for yourself. I'm just letting you know that big goals helped me feel like a warrior, like I was invincible, and proved my victimizers didn't win. For you, it might make you feel empowered to begin allowing yourself to trust others for the first time since your trauma occurred. It might be changing how you dress and care for your hair. Many people who experience trauma, particularly sexual trauma, stop taking care of their bodies and purposefully make themselves look frumpy, either because they think it'll decrease the chances of getting re-victimized or because they think they are disgusting, and their outward appearance is an expression of their inner self-loathing.

As you start setting and achieving goals in one aspect of your life, the benefits will naturally improve other aspects of your life. When you begin to feel better and more optimistic, you'll be able to set larger goals and eventually goals that create a larger vision and purpose for your life. However, don't worry about finding a purpose for your life right away, especially soon after your trauma occurs or soon after you begin processing past trauma for the first time. It will be difficult to look beyond your suffering in the early stages of healing, but the point is that by setting your sights on smaller wins, those wins accumulate over time and give you the hope and confidence to continue moving forward and seek out improvements in other aspects of your life.

You will always achieve whatever target you aim for. If you aim for nothing, that's exactly what you'll get. On the other hand, if you aim to make incremental improvements in your life and aim for goals that aren't dictated by your unchangeable past, over time, you'll find yourself in the life you desire and deserve. However, you can't get a new life without aiming for it and taking steps to achieve it. The next activity will allow you to start setting your sights on a different life.

Activity

Experiencing a different life will require a different version of you. Get out your journal and write down the mantra, "Old ways won't open new doors." You may also want to write it on a notecard or piece of paper and put it where you'll regularly see it. Before you can break free from the trap trauma has you in, remind yourself that what you've been doing is not going to allow you to break free. Changing how you're currently experiencing life requires that you change how you think and act each day. Of course, you can't change everything overnight, but you can decide at any moment to change.

Any time I'm looking to make a change in my life, I listen to YouTube videos and audiobooks by the late business philosopher, Jim Rohn. He often said, "The same wind blows on us all; the winds of disaster, opportunity and change. Therefore, it is not the blowing of the wind, but the setting of the sails that will determine our direction in life." The purpose of this activity, and ultimately of this book, is to help you set a better sail. To do that requires you to take different steps than you have been up to this point.

To begin, pick one area of your life to work on first. You don't want to start working on too many aspects of life at first, or you'll get overwhelmed, give up, and end up staying where you are. If you're not sure where to start, I encourage you to pick one area of your health. It'll be difficult for you to do well in any aspect of your life if you don't feel well, so improving your health is the quickest way to positively influence any aspect of your life. You could choose to improve your sleep, food or fluid intake, exercise, or emotional health.

Write in your journal the one area of your life you're going to work on first and what steps you're going to take each day to work toward this goal. For example, if you want to improve your sleep, you could go to bed 30 minutes early, stop looking at all electronic devices at least 30 minutes before you go to bed, or stop drinking any caffeinated beverage at least six hours before you go to bed. If you want to increase your water intake, you could swap out one cup of juice or soda each day for a cup of water, or you could purchase a bottle with the specific volume of water you want to drink each day and carry it around with you so you can monitor throughout the day how close you are to reaching your water intake goal. If you want to improve your emotional health, you could determine what people you want to spend more or less time with, determine a specific boundary you want to set with people regarding what you will and will not tolerate from them, or determine a boundary you want to set with yourself. For example, you may commit to stopping yourself or apologizing to yourself if you catch yourself saying something negative about yourself.

Goal setting has been so critical in my healing journey that I wrote an entire book on the topic. *Reclaim Your Life After Trauma: The Power of Goal Setting* details all facets of the goal setting process, including how to work through the habits, behaviors, and beliefs that are most likely to keep you stuck in the past. However, I think it is essential for you to know now that changing how you're currently experiencing life will be difficult. Even though you've experienced trauma, you are where you are right now because of the actions and thought patterns you've used to survive in the aftermath. Of course, I don't say this to hurt or make you feel bad for where you currently are in life. It sucks that you've had to endure what you have, and it sucks that trauma derailed your life.

However, only we can do the work to change our life after we experience trauma. Yes, others can help us, but they can't do the work for us.

As I've said before, every thought, behavior, and habit we have, we have because it has served us in some way. So, if we are stuck in habits and thought patterns, it's important to remember that we have them because they helped us survive in some way. Nevertheless, there always comes a point when unhealthy coping strategies and thought patterns become more harmful than beneficial. Still, even if these patterns are no longer serving us like they once did, there is comfort in old patterns. Our brain goes on high alert when we start making changes in our life, even if those changes are good for us. From an evolutionary standpoint, this makes complete sense, because changes in our internal and external environment could signal that our life is in danger. This is why all animals, including humans, are sensitive to changes in their environment. However, with our big and beautifully complex brains, us humans can easily interpret the messages of worry and anxiety in our brain as danger signals telling us to turn back; when really, those messages are just telling us to be on guard. Nonetheless, the moment some people start to feel a little afraid, they turn back instead of progressing forward, thinking it's too dangerous.

This is why it takes courage to move forward even when your brain and body are telling you that you might get hurt. It's important to remember that your brain and body can't predict the future. They don't know for sure whether the direction you're heading will be good or bad for you. All they know is that something is different, and danger can come with different. This is why people get nervous when they try something new. As human beings, it's natural to experience these emotions; however, many people perceive them as evidence that they should avoid making any changes. This underscores the importance of utilizing our incredible cognitive abilities to navigate the process of transformation. We must actively reassure ourselves about the reasons behind our decisions and the essential role that change plays in leading us towards a more fulfilling existence.

Not only is pivoting difficult, but the greater the change you're trying to make, the more resistance you're going to face. Chunk down your goals into bite-size pieces to minimize the worry and anxiety you'll face all at once, and you'll experience wins faster, which will encourage you to keep moving forward. This initial forward movement and collection of small wins will help build momentum.

Even with momentum and a collection of wins, you're not always going to feel motivated to do the work necessary to change your life. It's normal to be excited to change in the beginning. That early excitement can be used to push through the initial resistance you'll face when making change. However, you're eventually going to get tired or frustrated, and you're not going to feel like doing the work. You're going make excuses for not having the daily discipline necessary to change how you experience life. At that point, it's easy to make excuses for not doing the work and to put it off for a day. Then, one day turns into two, then three, and you eventually find yourself right back where you started. This means you need to force yourself to do the necessary work even when you don't feel like it.

One tool I've found particularly helpful is Mel Robbins' 5 Second Rule.[6] You can use the technique whenever you don't feel like taking a necessary action, such as getting out of your comfortable bed, putting your sneakers on to go for a walk or run, or filling your stomach with a cup of water before you decide to eat a sweet treat. Like a rocket launch, you simply count down, "Five, four, three, two, one," and then take off. Whenever I want to hit the snooze button, I say to myself, "Five, four, three, two, one," and sit up in the middle of my counting. The five-second rule is great for helping you act when you're scared or just don't feel like acting.

There are several factors that can contribute to you not wanting to act even when you made a commitment to yourself to do so. One factor can be that the activities needed to reach big goals are usually boring. That means we need to repeatedly remind ourselves why we're pursuing our chosen goal, so we can remember why we must continually push through the necessary mundane tasks.

You may also hesitate to take necessary action because you don't feel deserving of changing your circumstances. You might feel that you deserve to suffer and to keep experiencing life the way you are. If so, becoming aware of this will help you change your circumstances. However, it'll mean forcing yourself to act even when you don't feel deserving. You don't want to wait to use the resources until you feel deserving; you want to use them, so you'll begin to feel deserving.

Another factor might be that part of you believes taking action won't matter. Part of you might believe your suffering will never end, so there is no point in acting. If this is the case, it's also important to first become aware that this is what is at play in your mind. Next, you could begin challenging that belief. To do this, you could listen to podcasts, audiobooks, and YouTube videos about people who have experienced similar circumstances and made it through. Seeing that your suffering won't last forever may motivate you to act.

Depression might also play a role. Depression can make you not want to take any action. It can cause fatigue and hopelessness, in which case, consider therapy and/or medication. Another way to fight the symptoms of depression is with activities that increase feel-good chemicals in your brain, like physical activity, laughing, and being in nature. The issue with these activities is that depression can make it difficult to even get yourself to do them. Seeking medical help can sometimes speed the process along.

Sometimes, you may hesitate to take action because you don't know where to begin. You may have all the tools to move and keep moving but don't know where to start. Once you get overwhelmed, you're less likely to act. In that case, start small. Pick one activity to try out. If it works, keep doing it. If it doesn't, then maybe your starting activity is too big. If so, break down the steps to reaching your big goal even further.

Another thing people often have trouble with is maintaining momentum once they start. It's one thing to stop something if it's not useful, but you also need to give it enough time to work. Having an accountability system in place can help. You can tell a family member or friend your goal and can ask to check in with them each day to report your progress. Knowing you'll be accountable to another person may help you act when you don't feel like it. I've also found that using a Google Doc or Sheet works to keep me accountable to myself because I can access them on my phone or computer. I put my small daily goals in a Google Doc or Sheet and then note each day whether I accomplished each task, like meditation, exercise, and drinking two liters of fluid.

You could also be setting yourself up for failure by the way you define success. How you define success can change over time. Successes in your early stages of healing are likely to differ widely years later. In my moments of deepest despair, I counted showering as a success. However, I now consider successes to be different, such as traveling to exotic destinations and engaging in adventurous activities like paragliding and ice climbing. Even if your successes appear to grow over time, it doesn't mean you should stop celebrating and appreciating what you may want to dismiss as trivial. Exercising, eating healthily, and not reacting in anger are all notable successes regardless of your stage of healing.

I encourage you to make a running list of your past successes to add to over time. You can use a notebook, a document, or a note taking app. It's a great way to build confidence and belief in yourself that you can achieve your goals. Whenever you're feeling down about yourself or are afraid of taking the next steps toward your goal, you can review your past successes to remind yourself that you can do hard things.

Reframing

Once we realize we'll never forget our trauma and never be the same as before our trauma, we have two choices. One is that for the rest of our life, we can suffer by continuing to focus on all that we've lost and will no longer be because of our trauma. I know this place well. I was in this mindset for many years. During those years, I was bulimic, had unprotected sex with strangers, and contemplated suicide daily because I thought the suffering would never end. I felt completely hopeless. But when I took advantage of our second option after experiencing trauma, everything changed.

Our second option is to recognize that the trauma occurred, and nothing can change that, and then to focus on what is within our control. We do have control over how we look at our trauma and the possibilities for our future, even though this terrible thing occurred. Once I started to focus on the strength and resiliency I needed to survive, and the empathy and compassion I have for others in pain, I saw options for my future. I saw a way out of my suffering. I won't pretend it was easy, but my life today is so much better than any past version. I no longer want to go back, because the life I live today far exceeds any life I had envisioned for myself. I know from experience that transforming after trauma is possible. Instead of getting your old self and old life back, you can become someone new, with an even better life. That's why the next, and final section, of this chapter covers post-traumatic growth, the pinnacle of trauma healing. For now, we'll focus on a tool that is critical in allowing you to heal and move beyond your suffering: reframing.

Reframing is about looking at our circumstances from a different point of view. Reframing allows us to focus on what we've gained from our trauma instead of on what we've lost and will no longer be. I know this can seem like an impossible task early in our healing journey, but as time goes on, it gets easier to see what we've gained from our trauma. Even if you're not yet at where you can see what you have gained or could gain from your trauma, there are ways to view your trauma that make the burden of those painful memories a little lighter.

Reframing isn't about lying to ourselves about what happened and how our trauma has affected us. Reframing is about changing the way we tell our story, to soften and make it easier to deal with. Some people think this requires pretending the trauma never occurred and absolving their victimizers of all wrongdoing. It doesn't mean that at all. For example, I had a woman in a workshop I was conducting talk about how ashamed she was for having an abortion after being raped at a party. She blamed herself for drinking and dancing and thought she could have done something to stop the assault. Then she blamed herself for being unable to emotionally handle carrying the child of her rapist. But she wasn't blaming her victimizer at all. She was telling her story in a way in which she shouldered all the blame for her trauma and the abortion. She had eliminated her perpetrator from her story. So, we worked on her reframing these beliefs about being wrong, and she started saying her abuser was wrong. I know I said in the last chapter that it's not healthy to focus on getting angry and blaming others, but I meant over the long term. She was destroying herself and didn't want to live any longer because of the guilt she had over something she thought she did. But she wasn't telling the full story. By the end of the activity, she was able to say, "You're right. I'm not the only one to blame." She had literally never thought about what happened to her from that perspective.

That's what reframing is all about; looking at a situation from a different perspective. Small shifts in how we view the same set of circumstances in a situation can release us from some of our anguish. Again, reframing isn't about lying to ourselves or changing what happened. It's about looking at what happened from a different viewpoint so it's easier to handle, and it makes us more resourceful, so we have options for moving forward.

If I'm going to live for decades more after my trauma, it's not useful to just think of how it destroyed me. It's not going to allow me to be successful in any aspect of my life. That's why I've had to shift how I look at my experiences, so I could experience the successes I have had and will continue to have even though I've experienced immense suffering.

This is a very harsh world, and none of us will escape its wrath. We're not going to leave this Earth untouched by trauma. So, if we hold on to the belief that we're forever marked, that we're forever going to suffer because of our trauma, then we could spend decades of our life suffering. My traumatic experiences began at nine years old. What if I live to 90? I don't want to spend the remaining eight decades of my life suffering. That's a horrible way to live, yet I know many people who do live their lives that way because they don't think they have a choice. But we do have a choice. Even though we cannot change what happened to us in our past, we can change how we think about our past.

When I began to focus on the strength, resilience, empathy, and compassion I gained from my traumas, the story of my past changed. When the story of my past changed, I changed. I now live a life I truly love and am grateful every day that I never gave up. Yes, I still struggle with bouts of depression from time to time. Yes, thoughts from my past still creep in. But neither debilitate me like they used to. I've developed ways to deal with my hard days, so they don't linger long.

A major purpose of the next activity, and of this book, is to help you look at your trauma and what you've done to survive in the aftermath differently. Again, it's not about changing what happened and what you've done to survive, because neither are possible. It's about changing how you think about your suffering and what you've done to cope, so you can get unstuck. The main reason we get stuck after trauma is because of how we think about what happened to us. As I've said, it sucks that we've had to endure so much pain, and it sucks that it's now on our shoulders to figure out how to get past it, but if we only focus on how much everything sucks, we're going to get stuck there. Focusing on the things we cannot change isn't useful. Yes, they may be true, but they're not useful thoughts to focus on. The point of reframing is to allow ourselves to think differently, to become more resourceful and feel like we have options for moving forward. We'll never be able to see a path forward if we stay immersed in feelings of sadness, anger, frustration, and resentment over all we've had to endure. Reframing can help turn those feelings around.

Activity

In the last chapter, you listed the limiting beliefs you have about your trauma, your timeline for healing, and how you'll never be the same again. In this activity, you'll work on reframing those beliefs. To do this, get out your journal and work through one belief at a time. Write your first limiting belief down and then proceed with listing at least one possible reframe for this belief to start. Ideally, you want to list three to five reframes for each belief because not every reframe will resonate with you. Listing multiple reframes will allow you to try different points of view to see which alternate ways of thinking you are most likely to accept. After you've written down at least one reframe for your first limiting belief, continue listing your additional limiting beliefs and possible reframes in your journal.

If you believe your trauma was your fault, some reframes could be, "I was doing the best I could to survive," or, "The person who hurt me is to blame." If someone else gave you a timeline for healing, a reframe could be, "They were just trying to get me to stop telling my story so they wouldn't be uncomfortable." If you think you should have healed sooner, a reframe could be, "I had a lot of hard things happen before the trauma and since, so it's no wonder I'm still suffering." If you believe it sucks that you'll never be the same again, a reframe could be, "Now I'll be able to experience life in ways I never could have before."

Once you're done with this, it's time to consider what you have gained or could gain from your trauma. I realize that even thinking something good could come from the most painful experiences of your life can seem utterly absurd at some points in our healing journey. If you're currently in that place, it's okay. I encourage you to at least read through the remainder of this activity, so you know it's available to you when your pain isn't so raw.

When you're ready, journal what you've gained from your trauma. Have you gained a deep sense of empathy and compassion for others in pain? Do you feel strong and resilient because of all you've faced and yet survived? Are you persistent and determined to achieve success because you never want your abusers to win?

If you're not at a place in your healing where you're able to clearly identify what you've gained, write down what you think you could gain in the future. It might be helpful to look at yourself as an objective observer. Think of yourself as a person you don't know who's experienced immense suffering. Do you see options for that person? It might also be helpful to think of people you know or have heard stories about who've overcome great odds. Think about what was possible for them and whether the same is possible for you.

If you're not yet able to say, "I am stronger, more resilient, in a more fulfilling career...," consider starting each statement with "I will" instead of "I am." For example, you could write, "*I will* come out stronger on the other side of my pain." Open your mind to possibilities. Don't stop with one statement. Write down multiple alternatives to the way you currently think. Your mind may not be ready to accept each new alternative. You're just trying to make yourself more resourceful. The point of this activity is to shift how you're looking at yourself and your past, so that instead of feeling depressed, you can feel hopeful about your future. It's about getting you unstuck.

Changing how we think is necessary to change how we're currently experiencing life, but changing how we think is difficult. We face resistance by the negative track we have on repeat in our mind any time we try to tell ourselves something different. It's this negative track that will be the most likely culprit in sabotaging any goals you set for yourself. That's why I dedicate a significant portion of my

Reclaim Your Life After Trauma book to reframing and how to break free from old patterns of thinking and behaving that keep you stuck in the past you're trying to escape from. I encourage you to read or listen to the book if you find yourself backstepping each time you try to make progress. This backstepping is likely caused by an old story you have on repeat in your mind about what is and is not possible for you given your life circumstances. As Bishop TD Jakes says in a commonly replayed clip from one of his sermons, "The real battleground is in your mind… Stop wasting your weapons on what people say because it is not what they say about you that matters, it is what you say about you that threatens your destiny. You will never be defeated by what they say about you. You will be defeated by what you say about you."

The beliefs we have about ourselves didn't start overnight, and they're not going to disappear overnight either. Your beliefs were anchored in your mind by consistent reminders from the outside world about how you're not good enough and repeating them in your mind. This is especially true if you've been traumatized by someone you love and were supposed to trust.

I grew up with family and friends who thought it was appropriate to tell me I would never amount to anything and call me stupid, shit-for-brains, chipmunk cheeks, and fat ass. I understand how difficult it can be to challenge beliefs others have about you. I started to believe the statements about me after hearing them so often, especially since they started when I was too young to think critically. It took years to understand that these people were looking to break me down to control me or were repeating things to me that they had heard said to themselves or someone they loved out of ignorance of a different way.

As children, we're surrounded by adults who haven't done the work to heal their wounds, so they perpetuate their traumas onto their children, students, and community members. But, as children, we can't see that they're hurting us because they've been hurt; we just take what they say about us as truth. Even if, as adults, we can look back on who hurt us with empathy and compassion and understand that they were doing their best given their circumstances, it doesn't take away the pain or limiting beliefs they helped to anchor in our mind.

On top of negative messaging from the people around us, society is constantly telling us the ways we're deficient so we buy their latest gadget or enroll in their program. Because our beliefs are anchored by constant insults and replaying those insults in our mind, it takes the constant replaying of new tracks in our mind to reprogram our thinking. That's why I regularly consume motivational and inspirational audio.

Listening to the stories of others can be helpful in breaking apart our current story. If you go to my website, *serotinouslife.com/help*, you can sign up for a list of my favorite books, videos, and articles on healing from trauma and coping with life's daily stressors. In the video section, you'll see a link for "Motivation and Inspiration." This will bring you to a YouTube playlist of some of my favorite motivational and inspirational speakers, many of which have overcome great hardship.

Before investing time and energy into consuming a lot of new information and ideas, it's important to decide that you want to change. Some people say they want to change and will take initial steps to make it look as though they want to change, when in reality they're not ready to leave their comfort zone. Even if their current comfort zone is uncomfortable, they may think it is more comfortable than the unknown future they're considering pursuing. This is why two people can read the same book, take the same class, or work with the same coach and experience completely different results if one person is ready to leave their comfort zone and the other is not.

If you don't want to change the way you're experiencing life, you're going to be resistant to any new ideas that challenge your way of thinking. That's why you must first decide whether you're sick and tired of experiencing life the way you are and whether you want to experience life in a different way. If you want to experience life differently, then you must be ready to think and act differently. Once you're ready, you'll be receptive to new ways of thinking and acting and more willing to take the steps necessary to change your life.

Once I decided I wanted to change my life, I devoured audiobooks and YouTube videos to infuse my mind with alternate ways of thinking and expand my horizons. From my years learning and teaching about the human body, I know that even though we may look dramatically different from one another on the outside, there are few differences on an anatomical, physiological, and DNA level on the inside. That means what is possible for one person, is possible for another. Listening to stories about individuals who have overcome tremendous adversity tells me that I can do the same, and you can too!

Even when you've decided you're ready to change and are receptive to new ideas, you're still going to struggle while changing. You're fighting against your brain, which goes on high alert when change occurs and the negative beliefs you acquired about yourself during your lifetime resurface. Listening to and reading motivational and inspirational stories can help rewire your brain and override your negative beliefs, but it'll take time and a lot of repetition of new thought patterns and activities to break free from the years of accumulated limiting beliefs you have about yourself, your capabilities, and what is possible for you.

Even though you may eventually free yourself from your old ways of thinking and behaving, it's important to know that remnants of these old patterns will linger and resurface when life has beaten you down again. That means, after you adopt new ways of thinking and behaving, you'll need to maintain the activities you did to break old habits, so the new patterns remain and the old ones don't resurface and take hold when life overwhelms you again in the future, because it will. I know this from experience.

After experiencing trauma after trauma from my childhood to mid-twenties, I had a reprieve. For about a decade, life eased up on me, and the only battles I had to fight were with memories of traumas and typical life stressors. Yes, these can be formidable opponents, but they're not typically as bad as experiencing the trauma itself and the weeks and months immediately following the trauma. However, there was a period of eight months that life walloped me with one extreme stressor after another from mid-2022 through early 2023. As stressors compounded, my PTSD and depression worsened, and I ended up turning to old negative coping strategies and having suicidal thoughts, none of which I had experienced that severely or persistently in over a decade. It made the compounding stressors worse that I'd stopped regularly doing what was most important to me in my healing journey. I stopped listening to daily motivational and personal development videos and audiobooks. I also stopped walking and hiking as often.

I didn't get through this difficult period until I regularly re-implemented the tools that had been most important to me: self-care, goal setting, and reframing. The tool that helped me get back on track the most was filling my mind with ways of thinking that were different from the ones currently keeping me stuck. I did this through listening to positive, uplifting books and videos. I encourage you to start building an arsenal of books, videos, and podcasts to listen to each morning to start your day off right, throughout the day, and especially when you feel yourself entering an unresourceful state. Yes, it may also be helpful to have people you can call when you get into a stuck state, but you can't count on someone being available to talk every time the need arises. Audio resources are portable, and you can access them wherever your phone is. I encourage you to download your favorite books, videos, and podcasts to your phone, so, even when offline, you always have access to positive words that can quickly lift your spirits and change your state.

Is Post-Traumatic Growth Possible?

I set my sights on traveling around the world at a young age, and my desire for exploration grew throughout my teens and twenties. I am now 41 and have traveled to multiple countries on five continents. However, my dreams of adventure were never understood by most of my family and friends growing up. I grew up in a small town in Upstate New York, where there was no diversity in skin color, religion, or ways of thinking. Because most people never leave, the kids I went to school with, our parents, and even our grandparents attended the same school. If not for our town bordering the state of Vermont and Canada, most people in our town would have never experienced another state or country.

Although I still have many family members and friends in my hometown who I love and respect, and the town has a lot of beauty, there were people and aspects of the culture that caused me to be repeatedly victimized and stifled my desire for growth and adventure. It makes sense that I'm regularly asked where my desire to travel came from. It doesn't make sense to most people, since no one in my youth had the aspiration, or at least the willingness, to share their desire to travel.

Not until adulthood could I reflect on where my desire for travel and adventure came from. I believe it correlates to the cruelty I experienced starting at a young age. In addition to the numerous sexual violations, being continuously told I was dumb and would never amount to anything, I was told there was no point to me going to college and that I was only good for reproducing. Thankfully, I've always had an optimistic outlook on life. I believe it was necessary to keep me alive. I was able to survive trauma after trauma because I always believed, even when I was a child, that there was more to life than just pain. I held on to the belief that not all people were cruel. This drove me to search for evidence of good people and beautiful experiences, which, with my willingness to dream about a different future, allowed me to survive even worse traumas during my teenage years, keeping me focused on getting out of my hometown. It allowed me to focus on my studies instead of the pain, and on my dreams for the future, despite being continually condemned for being an idealistic dreamer. My quest for something more and for something different from what I had been exposed to my whole life drove my desire for adventure and exploration. Once I graduated high school and left my hometown for college, I learned that my instincts had been correct all along.

Yes, I still encountered people who hurt me and painful circumstances when I left my hometown, but I could now choose not to spend time with people who hurt me and to engage in new experiences to help negate my bad experiences. Because colleges, particularly ones with dorms, bring people together from different locations and backgrounds, you have a selection of people to spend your time with. People rarely leave my hometown. When they do, they rarely come back, and new people rarely come in, so the town is a collection of people with similar ways of thinking or who have been willing to stifle their different views to fit in with the pack. This means everywhere in my hometown I turned, and almost everyone I spoke to, hurt me with the same types of words and actions I had been exposed to for my whole existence there. People were just recycling their pain and ways of thinking because there were no new ways of thinking to stop those cycles.

It's important to note that I'm not condemning my hometown or the people in it. Again, many people I love and care about still live there. However, I cannot forget that I was tormented my entire life there by people's words, actions, and inactions. I experienced the same types of abuse and neglect over and over because most people thought and acted the same. It's also important to note that what I experienced is not unique to my hometown. It happens in all small towns and tight-knit communities in big cities. It happens anytime you have a collection of people who don't regularly interact with different types of people with different ways of thinking and behaving. This is why I'm such a strong advocate for young people who grow up in these types of communities to either go away to college; volunteer in different towns, states, or countries; or listen to and read stories of people from different walks of life. The moment I was exposed to different people and circumstances, my life changed.

This first happened when I went to Upward Bound during the summer between my freshman and sophomore year in high school. Upward Bound prepares low-income, first-generation high school students for college. During the program, you spend six weeks on a college campus, taking courses, living in the dorms, participating in team building activities, and volunteering. I loved it so much, I participated in Upward Bound for three years.

It was the exact experience I needed to open my mind to new possibilities for my future. Over the first two summers, I met people from other parts of Upstate New York, and during the third summer, I met people from all over the world because I participated in a different type of Upward Bound program. This exposure to different people with different ways of thinking and behaving expanded my horizons. This expansion was compounded by the exposure to different courses, and team building and volunteer activities that I participated in each summer. It proved I was right all along, that there was more to life than pain and suffering. There were people who wouldn't hurt me. There were unlimited opportunities for my future.

When I was able to leave my hometown after graduation to go to college, these beliefs and opportunities for my future continued to grow. As my mind opened further to new possibilities, I saw that not only could I move beyond my traumas, but I could use them to propel me forward. I used every hateful word and action, every unwanted touch, and every dismissal of me, my feelings, and goals for my future as fuel to achieve everything I was told I couldn't or that people tried to take from me.

I was told not to bother going to college, because my only purpose was to reproduce, so I spent 12 years in college, earning three degrees, including a doctorate. I was told I was stupid and would never amount to anything, so I became a college professor teaching difficult science topics and ultimately an author and business owner. I was treated again and again as unlovable and like my only value was through sex and reproducing, so I found a tribe of people who truly love me and feel that I have immense value beyond my body. These are all examples of ways I've experienced post-traumatic growth.

The purpose of this chapter is to give you not only the tools for envisioning a version of your life where you're not hobbled by trauma, but also to see that you're stronger because of the pain you've endured. Post-traumatic growth is the experience of positive changes in one's life after trauma. The point of this section of the book is to allow you to begin dreaming again, to start to make meaning from your suffering, and to find a purpose for your life.

As I said in the last section, I realize in early stages of our healing that the possibility of experiencing something good from the most devastating experience of our life can seem absolutely absurd. Traumatic events are deeply disturbing and challenge our feelings of safety and beliefs about the world around us. So, if you're still in that deep, dark place where you feel your trauma has swallowed you whole, I understand that this section may be difficult for you. Please meet yourself where you're currently at. If you need to skip this section, then skip it. But I encourage you to try to read it now, so you know what is possible for your future, even if the thought isn't fully accessible to you right now. It is possible for you to make meaning from your suffering. I have, and as I've said before, what is possible for one human being is possible for another. You deserve to experience a beautiful life, regardless of how ugly your past has been, and the life you desire will be there for you when you're ready to reach for it. The next activity will help you envision your new life.

Activity

Get out your journal and begin crafting a vision for your future. Where do you want to live? Be specific. Identify what country, state, and city or town you want to live in. What do you want your home to look like? If you like where you currently live, identify why so you can be clear about the parts of the vision for your life that you have already realized.

What do you want to do for a career? Are you already in your dream job or business? If not, what does your dream career look like? If you're already retired, are you enjoying your days? If so, identify what you are enjoying and anything else you would like to do to improve your quality of life.

Do you have any travel dreams or adventures, or new experiences you would like to have?

What does your ideal financial situation look like? What income do you want each month or year? How much do you want in savings? What about the amount of debt you have?

What does your ideal health look like? How would you look and feel physically, mentally, and emotionally?

What do your relationships look like? Which relationships do you want to keep, which do you want to end, and what new ones would you like to pursue in the future? Are there certain qualities you're looking for in the people you want to attract into your life? How will and will they not treat you?

How do you want to contribute to your family, friends, community, and world at large? Do you want to volunteer your time, donate money, write a book, or start a nonprofit organization?

If you're having difficulty with this activity, think about dreams and goals you had before your trauma. What did you want to do or experience when you were a child, before the world stifled your creativity and dreams? What have others done or achieved that made you say, "Wow," and wish you could do the same? What would make you feel like you won and that your trauma didn't break you?

Even if you don't think your current dreams are possible right now, write them down. It'll be normal for your nagging inner critic to come out and play during this activity just to tell you you're crazy for dreaming so big and that you'll never be able to accomplish this beautiful vision for your future. These are voices from your past or people in your present life who are not happy in their own life, so they pass their pain onto others so they're not alone in their misery. The voice of your nagging inner critic is the voice of every negative and cruel person you've ever encountered. Although you may repeat what it says out loud, and part of you might believe what it says, it's important to start recognizing that these negative stories in your head were given to you by others. The only way to override them is with new stories. A vision board can serve as a constant reminder that there is more to life than pain and suffering. It's about envisioning a life that isn't marred by your trauma. As you begin to take ownership of the future you have envisioned for yourself, it'll be easier to ignore the nagging inner critic and tell it to shut up when necessary.

I chose Serotinous Life as the name for my business because it's my mission to help fellow trauma survivors reach the holy grail of trauma healing, post-traumatic growth. I named my business after serotinous cones, which only release their seeds when exposed to an environmental trigger, such as fire or the death of the parent plant. People often only focus on how destructive fires can be or how sad death is, but trees with serotinous cones require these forms of devastation for their cones to open and release their seeds. Without these extreme stressors, new life would not follow, and their species would eventually die out.

This is similar to our body in many ways. Our muscles won't strengthen unless we stress them. Muscles require microtrauma — small tears — to stimulate their growth. Our brain needs to be challenged by new information and experiences to develop more neural connections. Our bones are particularly fascinating. Not only do bones get stronger with the more stress you place on them, but when they experience the most serious type of stress, a break, the bone grows thicker and stronger around where the bone was broken. This prevents the bone from breaking in the same way again in the future. The same applies to us. Each time we experience stress, or are broken by trauma, we also grow back stronger so we can handle similar difficult situations in the future without breaking in the same way.

It's easy to think that we'll never be able to pick up our broken pieces after we experience trauma. Yes, the process of doing so will be long and difficult, and our pieces will never fit back together in the same way they did before, but that's why I liken trauma healing to *kintsugi*, the Japanese art of repairing broken pottery with a precious metal. When the broken pieces are bound back together with gold, silver, or platinum, the pottery often looks more beautiful than it did before it was broken. The same can be true for us.

Even though we may not be able to go back to being the person we were before, we can become an even better version of ourselves. Our traumas may cause us to rethink our lives and shift in a different direction. Shifting requires a different version of ourselves, a transformation. I titled my first book *Transformation After Trauma* because that's what I've found is truly possible after trauma — a transformation. After experiencing trauma, we can become someone we never were before. We can create a life for ourselves that is even better than the one we had or had envisioned for ourselves before our trauma. I no longer want to go back to any version of my past life, because my life gets better every year. This only could have happened by me letting go of the person I was. The process wasn't easy, but the time, energy, and heartache along the way were worth it. Please try to hold on to the belief that the same will be true for you.

Chapter 5

Do I Need to Forgive?

The deep feeling of sadness and despair is always palpable in the people who ask me, "Do I need to forgive my perpetrator to heal?" Hearing this question always sends me back to all the times people tried to dictate to me how I should heal. All the world seems to be an expert on how to live your life, even when they have no idea about your life circumstances. Even when they do, they may come at you with an air of superiority as they lecture you on what you need to do to move on. My need to forgive and forget has spewed like projectile vomit from the mouths of numerous people who thought they had the right to dictate to me what I needed to do to work through the pain someone else caused me.

The concept of forgiveness involves letting go of anger and resentment toward those who have harmed you. It makes sense that thoughts of anger and resentment keep you stuck and removing them from your mind makes room for positive thoughts. The less you're dragged down by negativity, the more resourceful you'll be. It makes sense to me that forgiveness is not for the person who hurt you but for your own benefit, but it infuriates me when it's delivered as an ultimatum or as if you are to blame for your own suffering because of your unwillingness to forgive the person who hurt you. These blanket statements that make forgiveness a necessity in healing from trauma neglect the complexity of trauma. Most people who spout their rules for trauma healing don't consider that one's trauma is much more than the event itself. The effects of trauma are compounded by one's experiences before the trauma. Past abuse, neglect, bullying, and other forms of hurtful actions or inactions can make the traumatic experience worse if the trauma reinforces painful experiences from the individual's past. The effects of trauma are also compounded by the ways trauma infiltrates every aspect of one's life. When you see pain everywhere you look because of your trauma, it isn't as easy as just stopping yourself from feeling anger and resentment; not when you can make a direct link between your current suffering and what someone else or a group of people did to you.

People who dictate the necessity of relieving ourselves of all anger and resentment fail to realize the immense pressure the concept of forgiveness places on us. In the early stages of my healing, this pressure made me feel like I was suffocating. Here I was already in a deep hole, and them spouting the necessity of forgiveness felt like they were shoveling dirt into the hole I was already in. It sucks enough that we must work to repair the damage someone else did to us, but it sucks even more when someone blames us for not moving faster through our healing because of our "unwillingness" to release our anger and resentment against those who harmed us. These people who place this pressure on us don't understand that trauma rips through our life like a tornado, flinging pieces of ourselves all over, destroying some and leaving others in places never to be found again. They don't understand that their rules for healing can further traumatize us or cause us to remain stagnant or regress in our healing.

Even though my anger and resentment have subsided, I'm not sure they'll ever fully disappear, and I'm not sure I want them to. Those who insisted I would never heal without forgiving my perpetrators dismissed the ways anger and resentment can be harnessed. I've accomplished so much since my traumas occurred, largely because of the way I harnessed my anger. It elicited the fighter in me, and that fighter refused to let my victimizers win. I refused to let circumstances outside of my control determine the trajectory of the rest of my life. That fire still burns inside me, and the sting of its flames prompts me into action, to keep accomplishing more and experiencing life to its fullest.

Although I want to continue to harness the residual anger I feel toward my perpetrators and what they've stolen from me, I don't want to continue to feel anger toward myself. Out of all the people we could forgive, I think we are the most important person to deliver our forgiveness to, in full. We must forgive ourselves for anything we think we should have done differently before, during, or after our trauma. We must realize that we were doing the best we could to survive, before, during, and after. As trauma survivors, it's easy to get caught up in an endless cycle of self-blame and shame, particularly over the coping mechanisms we've acquired. As I continue to say, trauma overwhelms our capacity to cope, so it makes sense to hold on to anything that offers a moment's relief from our suffering and painful memories, such as food, drugs, alcohol, or sex. We must always remember that we were doing the very best we could to survive and to regain the sense of control we lost during our trauma.

I used to be so ashamed of my self-destructive behaviors, particularly the promiscuity and the vomiting after stuffing myself with enormous amounts of food. As time passed after my traumas, I began to understand that I was doing these things to survive and recapture the control I lost during my traumas. I was able to remember how often I contemplated suicide when my self-destructive behaviors were at their worst, and I saw how the promiscuity and eating disorder actually saved my life. These were critical reframes for me. Instead of seeing these behaviors as disgusting and shameful, I started looking at them with immense gratitude for saving my life. No part of me views this as an overstatement. I gorged myself with food just to vomit it up and found another random man to sleep with when I was barely clinging to existence. These activities distracted me from wanting to take my own life long enough for me to determine that I wanted to live and figure out a way to stop destroying myself. This shift in how I thought about these coping strategies helped release the increasing shame and hatred I felt toward myself.

Even though others can be harsh to us, we are often harsher to ourselves. Sometimes the most hurtful words are from us. It hurts when someone we care about and are supposed to trust hurts us with their words, but it also hurts when we aim hurtful words at ourselves. The words we use to condemn ourselves often send us on a loop of destructive thoughts or activities that then cause us to resent ourselves further, and so the cycle continues.

Once I started to forgive myself, I saw that some level of forgiving my perpetrators was possible. I'm now able to see that they hurt me because of the ways they had been hurt. But some of them were so cruel in their treatment of me, that I may never fully absolve them of their wrongdoing. The only people I've reserved full forgiveness for are those working to heal the wounds that caused them to hurt me. Ultimately, forgiving your perpetrators is a highly personal decision. Society tells us that we *must* forgive our perpetrators to heal. After being treated so atrociously by so many people, I just don't believe that's true. But I do believe that we must reach a point where we can think about our perpetrators in a way that allows us to move forward. That may include forgiveness, but it may not. It may include harnessing our anger against our perpetrators, but it may not. What's important is that we don't allow the people who have hurt us in the past to continue to hurt us by recycling in our mind the pain they caused us. This is where reframing can help you develop ways to think about what others have done to you, so you don't remain stuck in the place they tried to keep you.

Regardless of what we choose to do about those who have harmed us, when it comes to us, we must do the work necessary to discontinue patterns of self-hatred and self-destruction. Are there patterns from our past we should avoid repeating? Of course. Are there ways that we have hurt ourselves or others while grasping for any hope for survival? Of course. However, the point is to learn from what you've done in the past, so you don't repeat past mistakes. There is a difference between remembering what you've done so you can learn from and not repeat it, and continuously beating yourself up for all the times you weren't at your best.

We must show ourselves compassion for all we've endured. It's no wonder we adopt some of the coping mechanisms we do when we consider all the collective experiences we've had in life.

It's easy to come up with a variety of ways we have been shamed and put down that weren't even directly related to our trauma. Those little insults to our dignity eroded our self-esteem and self-worth. Combine these accumulated insults with our trauma, and it's easy to see how we can fall into a pit and grasp at anything to help us survive while we feel forever trapped. That's why it's necessary to practice empathy, compassion, and forgiveness for ourselves, for all the ways we've tried to survive.

Activity

Journal and identify the things you need to forgive yourself for. Do you need to forgive yourself for harming yourself with drugs or alcohol, overeating or undereating, overexercising, or overworking? Do you need to forgive yourself for harming others while trying to cope with your stress? Do you need to forgive yourself for not being more present with your family and friends or for not taking better care of yourself?

If you're having difficulty forgiving yourself for any of the things you've written down, I encourage you to practice reframing them. How can you look at what you've done a little differently to make it easier to handle? What can you tell yourself to show yourself empathy, compassion, and kindness, instead of anger and shame, when you beat yourself up over what you've done in the past or for falling back into old patterns? To do this, it may help to think about what you gained from each of these things. For example, did saying hurtful words to someone else make you feel like you had power and that you were in control, or did it make you feel like you were compensating for being unable to stand up to your abusers? If you engaged in self-harming behavior, did it give you a moment's relief or distraction from your suffering, or did it make you feel good, even if for a moment?

There have been days in your past and there will be days in your future when you're not at your best and you may hurt yourself or others, but please try to remember that you're doing the very best you can given your circumstances. In the documentary *Cracked Up: The Darrell Hammond Story*, trauma researcher Dr. Bessel van der Kolk said, "The most important thing is forgiveness of yourself, for having been as vulnerable, as scared, as angry, as frozen as you were. And forgiving yourself for all the ways you've tried to survive." He acknowledged, "That's a big job."[7] Even though it won't always be easy, forgive yourself when you're not at your best and apologize to others if you cause them pain, but treat each day as a new beginning — another chance.

Chapter 6

How Can I Cope With Guilt?

A big reason it's important to work on forgiving yourself is so you can work through any feelings of guilt you have for what you think you should or shouldn't have done before, during, or after your trauma. In the reframing section in Chapter 4, I discussed the workshop attendee who blamed herself for the night she got raped at a party and blamed herself for not being able to handle carrying the baby her assailant left her with. Having an abortion filled her with immense guilt. In addition to discussing how she could use reframing to help shift the shame she was carrying onto the shoulders of her assailant, we also discussed how she could think differently about the unbearable guilt she was carrying from having an abortion.

We discussed how society blames the victim. We also discussed how certain sections of society place immense pressure on women to not have an abortion, but they don't give a crap about the emotional health of the woman carrying the physical product of her rape in addition to hidden scars in the form of indelible memories. This was a young girl, and she was still trying to cope with being raped and couldn't also handle figuring out how to be a mom. She had her whole life in front of her. Before her rape, she was focusing on her educational goals and future career. After her rape, she felt faced with giving her life up to have a child that would bear the face of the man who stole her life from her. Her perpetrator put her in an impossible situation. Given the time constraints of a pregnancy and an abortion, she had very little time to make a decision.

The guilt this young woman experienced is understandable when viewing her situation as an observer. Whether or not the blame was appropriately assigned, she felt she could have done something to prevent her rape, so it's expected that she would extend that blame to any consequences of the rape, including a pregnancy. Most societies still blame women for their rape. The shame society associates with abortion entirely falls on the woman, with her body able to carry a child and a man never able to, even though a child cannot be made without both parties present. That's why it's no wonder she bore the burden of shame and guilt with these compounding pressures and condemnation from society. Combine that with her need to feel some form of control over her rape, and it makes complete sense that she got stuck in these unresourceful thought patterns.

When discussing the commonality of the guilt trauma survivors face in her book, *Trauma and Recovery*, psychiatrist Dr. Judith Lewis Herman said, "To imagine that one could have done better may be more tolerable than to face the reality of utter helplessness."[3] This is why guilt is common with most forms of trauma. If you were physically, sexually, or verbally assaulted, it's expected that you will try to grasp for some way that you were to blame so you feel like you did have and still have some form of control. It's why it's normal to experience guilt when you are able to live and move on with your life after the loss of a loved one. Survivor guilt is also very common in times of war and other tragedies like pandemics and school shootings.

Losing my partner at 25 was one of the hardest things I've ever experienced. It took years to not think about my loss daily. In the early years, sadness filled me every time I thought about Stan. I thought about what I lost and what would no longer be because he was no longer in my life. I struggled with pangs of guilt whenever I even thought of moving on with my life. Here he is, no longer alive, and I'm getting the opportunity to move forward and experience life in ways he now won't be able to.

It's now been over 15 years since Stan passed. I still think about him, but not as frequently. When I do, I'm not filled with the immense sadness like in the beginning. If you still struggle with daily, gut-wrenching heartache over your loss, please know that it will get easier. It'll take time and requires you to shift how you think about your loss, but with enough time and shift in perspective, your pain will lessen like it has for me.

What helped me to begin moving beyond the pain of my loss and associated guilt was to start focusing on different things when I thought about Stan. Instead of remaining focused on all that I lost, I focused on the beautiful experiences I was blessed to have with him. I focused on the fact that nothing is permanent in our lives including our life. All we ever have is this one moment, so I focused on being grateful for the moments I did have with him while he was with me on Earth. Whenever sadness filled me, I shifted that by thinking about a happy memory of him, something that made me smile. Yes, sometimes it made me miss him more, but over time, I was able to sit with the beautiful memories and focus on the gratitude I had for being able to experience those times with him. Those memories no longer fill me with sadness, but with happiness.

When I started to move forward and find someone new, I had to fight my desire to compare the other person to Stan. After Stan died, I made him into much more than he was. The picture I'd made of him became distorted. Yes, he loved me in ways I had never experienced. Yes, he always did his best to make me smile. Because I tried so hard to focus on the beautiful times in our relationship, over time, I suppressed the not-so-good parts. With him being an alcoholic, I had to deal with the constant stench of vodka on his breath and regularly watching him have difficulty standing up. With him being a drug addict, I had to experience giving him CPR while waiting for the ambulance to come when he almost died from a heroin overdose. With him being on life parole, I had to deal with visits to my home from his parole officer, which included his parole officer treating him like crap and ridiculing me for being with him.

After he died, all these difficulties in our relationship vanished from my mind. By the time I started dating again, I had put Stan on a pedestal that was almost impossible for any other man to reach. However, in reality, he wasn't as perfect as I had made him out to be in my mind after he died. So, when I started dating again, I had to remind myself I would never be able to replicate what I had lost with him; that I would never find a man who made me feel the same way. But I allowed myself to focus on the possibility that I could have an even better relationship going forward.

This was a crucial shift in perspective for me. It allowed me to stop clinging to the idealized version of Stan and the life I thought I was going to have with him. It allowed me to see that an early death was inevitable for him and that I would have experienced more pain the longer we were together. I eventually got to the point where I could see how his loss was good for me. I know some people may shudder when they read those words and think about me expressing gratitude for losing a man I loved, but it's the potential condemnation from others that makes me and others in similar situations hesitant to even think about the benefits we could gain from losing a loved one and other forms of trauma, let alone stating those benefits out loud. However, I think it's important that I write my truth to give you the power to speak your own truth and dissolve the shame that has been cultivated by silence, secrecy, and the fear of being judged.

Dr. Brené Brown studies shame and vulnerability. In her book, *Daring Greatly*, she said, "Shame derives its power from being unspeakable... If we cultivate enough awareness about shame to name it and speak to it, we've basically cut it off at the knees. Shame hates having words wrapped around it. If we speak shame, it begins to wither. Just the way exposure to light was deadly for the gremlins, language and story bring light to shame and destroy it."[8] Therefore, when you're completing the following activities in this book, revisiting the activities you've already done, and when you're reflecting on your trauma in the coming weeks, months, and years, I encourage you to name the things you're afraid to say. You don't need to say it to anyone else, and you don't need to write it down. But at least allow yourself to think certain thoughts without condemning yourself for it or quickly distracting yourself from letting those thoughts grow in your mind. Sometimes it's the things we're unwilling to say that give us the most freedom when we break the silence and allow the shame to wither and die. Everything changed for me the moment I was able to acknowledge, without guilt, the benefits Stan's death provided me. Let me be clear: this does not mean I'm glad he's gone and that I regret any time I spent with him, because neither are true. It just means I can look at his loss in a way that no longer traps me. Again, that's the point of reframing. It's about making you more resourceful. It's not about changing what happened. It's about changing how you think about what happened.

The next activity gives you the opportunity to create some reframes for the ways you feel guilty about your trauma. Like with all reframing, the hope is that shifting your perspective will make you feel less stuck and as though you have more options for moving forward.

Activity

Journal what about your trauma you feel guilty about. For example, if you were attacked, do you blame yourself for not fighting back? Or do you have survivor's guilt?

Proceed with writing one or more reframes for each of the things you feel guilty about. If you blame yourself for not fighting back, could you have saved your life or prevented further injury by not fighting back? If you feel guilty for surviving, could this be your opportunity to live the remainder of your life in honor of the person who is no longer living?

You may end up writing down some of the same things or similar things as in the activity in the reframing section of Chapter 4. That's okay; write them down again. Even if you've already practiced reframing those thoughts, it's good to do it again now that some time has passed. You've taken in additional information and had time to reflect. This may allow reframes to come to mind that you hadn't previously considered. You might find that you're now willing to accept a reframe you previously dismissed, or one of your new reframes might quickly resonate with you.

Losing a loved one changes us. Our needs when we were with our partner who passed may no longer be the same once we start to pick up the pieces and move on. Once we no longer have our partner — a person who may have been an extension of ourselves — it takes time to explore the new version of ourselves. When they died, part of us died with them. This means we will be different moving forward, and our needs from a new partner may be different. This means that it's okay for us to have somebody in our life who's different from our partner who has passed.

After Stan died, I had to continually remind myself that even though part of me died with him, I was still here in body and spirit. I had the opportunity to survive, and because of that, I cannot squander the gift of continued life I was given just because he wasn't given that same gift. I now choose to live my life fully to honor the life that he lost.

The same is true if you feel that you lost part of yourself when your trauma occurred. With many traumas, part of us dies, never to be reclaimed again. It's natural to grieve that loss. It's natural to wish it never happened and that you could have done something to prevent it. However, it's important that you eventually acknowledge that part of you is gone and there is nothing you can do to change it. Yes, it sucks that your life was uprooted and you must make these acknowledgments, but those acknowledgments must be made just the same. It's okay if you're not quite ready to. It's okay if a lot of time passes before you are ready. Don't push yourself farther or faster than you're ready. Eventually, you'll reach a point where your wounds aren't as tender and the memories aren't always at the front of your mind. When this begins, you'll start to see the possibilities in front of you instead of only focusing on what's behind you.

I encourage you to honor the part of yourself that died with your trauma by not allowing the rest of you to die along with it. Your pain won't be relieved overnight, and the memories will always creep in, but you can live a life that isn't dictated by what was taken from you and what you feel you deserve because of the shame, blame, and guilt you've shouldered. This is your opportunity to unload some of that weight.

Chapter 7

How Do I Trust Again?

After experiencing multiple traumas, I never thought I would be able to mend my broken pieces. I thought I would never feel whole again. I thought I would always feel like I could never trust anyone and would never have healthy relationships. It turns out none of that was true! I no longer feel broken; I feel stronger than ever! I now have many loving relationships and living a life I never thought was possible. I've committed that life to helping others who also feel they'll never be able to mend their broken pieces. One of the most important obstacles I needed to overcome to get to this place was learning, and being willing, to trust again.

Trust can be broken when someone we were supposed to trust hurts us with their actions or inactions. It's bad enough when someone we care about hurts us directly with their words or actions, but it can be equally painful when someone we depend on doesn't come to our aid when we need them. That's why psychiatrist Dr. Judith Lewis Herman said in her book, *Trauma and Recovery*, "When trust is lost, traumatized people feel that they belong more to the dead than to the living."[3] I know this feeling well. For most of the years of my life, I felt disconnected from people. Part of that disconnection was purposeful because I didn't want to get hurt again, but part was because I didn't feel like I fit anywhere. People have always preferred to see the happy, bubbly Stephanie and not the sad, depressed Stephanie. People who are consumed with their own suffering can't expend energy on mine. Even though I understand this on an intellectual level and can empathize with others' suffering, it still erodes my faith in those who are unable to be with me when I'm desperately reaching out for connection.

Because hurt people hurt people, and people who are hurting are limited in their capacity to be with others and their suffering, it's no wonder learning how to trust again is one of the biggest concerns I hear from my readers, social media followers, and clients. Most think it's an unattainable goal. Most think the only way to get through life is to armor up, build impenetrable walls around them, and not let anyone close enough to hurt them again. However, the same walls we build to keep out pain also keep out love, and love is one of the best antidotes for emotional pain. I said this on a social media post, and a lot of people agreed. However, I also had a lot of people disagree, saying things like, "Love also causes emotional pain." Of course, both statements are true. Love can be a mixed blessing. Allowing ourselves to be vulnerable and love another person opens us up to getting hurt. At the same time, vulnerability and love can be used to heal past wounds caused by other people. Because most of my traumas were caused by other people, I didn't allow myself to get close to others for much of my life. But everything changed once I started to let people in. I just had to make sure I had the self-care tools to handle getting hurt again once I decided to allow myself to be vulnerable with others.

The reason people are afraid to trust and need to have a plan in place to handle getting hurt again in the future is because there are great costs that come from loving another. I have paid dearly for loving people who ultimately caused me tremendous pain. People pass their pain along to others, which means we are in a world filled with people who are in pain and transmitting it to others, and so the cycle goes.

Even though I've paid dearly for allowing people to get close to me, I've also paid dearly during the significant period of my life I chose not to get close to others because of the ways I've been hurt. Even though we can pass our pain onto others, we can also pass on happiness, joy, and love. Happy, loving people can transmit their happiness and love to us. We can then pass that onto others instead of pain and misery. I find that when someone smiles at me or holds the door, I have the desire to do the same for someone else. When we choose to love and be vulnerable, there is a risk of both being hurt and experiencing enrichment. However, if we decide not to love at all, we always miss out on the opportunity to be enriched by others.

Humans are deeply social creatures. We're not able to make it through life without depending on other people. Believe me, I tried for years to prove this wasn't true, but I ultimately failed. Because allowing ourselves to be vulnerable enough to love another person is so hard, especially after being hurt, it's essential we have tools in place to handle being hurt. During the years I tried to be as independent as possible, so I wouldn't need another person, I knew I wasn't ready or able to pay the price of getting hurt again. I knew I needed to prevent people from getting in because I was barely holding on, and any additional pain could push me over the edge. I needed to do a tremendous amount of healing and develop several coping mechanisms to handle the inevitable ways people would hurt me again before I was willing to let others close to me. Now that I've developed tools to handle the ways people will hurt me, I'm able to pay the hefty fee associated with allowing myself to be vulnerable enough to love again. You can get to that point too.

The first step was for me to develop coping strategies to deal with getting hurt. The self-care and reframing tools you started to develop in Chapter 4 will help you in this portion of your healing journey. Self-care tools and changing how we think about what someone says or does to us are essential to handling the unavoidable ways people will hurt us.

The next step toward allowing people to get close to me was to choose who to let in. When we've been hurt by others, we're not just going to one day be able to allow everyone into our lives. With how toxic some people are, I believe there are people we should never let close to us. I think it's necessary to always be selective with who we let in, but we can't be so selective that we never let anyone in. A common limiting belief I hear is, "I can't trust anyone." I used to say the same myself. I truly believed no one could ever be trusted. I believed this in part because I surrounded myself with people who couldn't be trusted. I needed to work on changing who I spent time with. Many who have experienced trauma think only those who've immensely suffered can understand their pain. In many ways this is true, but many people who've experienced immense suffering go on to hurt others because they haven't done the difficult task of working through their pain in healthy ways. Although many of my closest friends today have experienced suffering like mine, they've also done, and are continuing to do, the work to heal their wounds in healthy ways.

During much of my early life, I gravitated toward individuals who tried to erase their pain with alcohol and drugs. Part of why I gravitated toward them is because I also used to believe you could only get through your pain by trying to erase it. It's why I used to regularly drink until I blacked out, but it's also why I've been sexually assaulted so many times. Many of these encounters involved me drinking, my perpetrator drinking or using drugs, or both of us being intoxicated.

A major step in my healing journey was to begin eliminating toxic people from my life. If someone can't take care of their own needs, how can they take care of ours? They can't. This is why it's a problem when broken souls bond over their brokenness. They identify with and feel like they understand one another, but neither is healthy enough to be an effective emotional support for the other. This results in them further hurting one another and further solidifying their belief that no one can be trusted or depended upon.

When I decided to eliminate toxic people from my life, I couldn't do it all at once. I began by cutting out the most obviously dysfunctional individuals. At that point, I didn't have anyone in my life who wasn't dysfunctional. I couldn't let go of everyone at once because, again, as humans, we crave human connection. As I began to eliminate the most dysfunctional individuals from my life, I got stronger because they were no longer hurting me with their words, actions, and inactions and were no longer there to encourage my self-destructive behaviors like drinking until I blacked out.

As I got stronger, I drew healthier people into my life as I started engaging in different activities. Instead of spending my free time at the bar, I went for walks and hikes with groups. This is where Meetup.com helped. Through this site, I searched for groups that interested me. Groups that did various outdoor activities attracted me, but you can find variety on there, like groups that go to movies, go out to eat, or discuss new books.

Meeting new people through these groups made me realize I didn't need to keep some of the dysfunctional people I still had in my life. As I replaced unhealthy activities and people with healthy ones, I got stronger, and the less I depended on unhealthy coping strategies, the less time I wanted to spend with unhealthy people. Even though I surrounded myself with healthier people, I kept them at arm's length. I spent several years in this stage. As I did more work on myself and spent more time on self-reflection, I realized the next step in my healing journey was to allow myself to get closer to people. Because I spend a lot of time listening to books on personal development, I grew aware of how certain behaviors of mine could be limiting me. I looked at my patterns, like not responding to phone calls, text messages, and emails, and realized they were partly to keep people at a distance. I believe it was my way of showing people I didn't need them and had a life that didn't involve them. Once I saw how I was sabotaging my friendships, I reflected on why. It ultimately came down to the fear of getting hurt again.

It's important to note that I could only get to this point of awareness because I regularly spend time in self-reflection and consuming books that deepen my look inward. A major purpose of this book is to make you pause and reflect on where you could be tripping yourself up in your healing. When we experience trauma, it's easier to point to outside factors for why we're struggling, but it's difficult to point at ourselves. The truth is that even though our trauma is what dropped us to our knees, we usually stay down long after being hobbled because of our own habits, behaviors, and beliefs. Yes, we may not have ever acquired our dysfunctional habits, behaviors, and beliefs without experiencing the trauma we did, but we can't change how we're experiencing life until we change the parts of our life that are keeping us stuck in our past. As I've said, yes, it sucks that we've experienced that pain, and it sucks it's on us to mend our broken pieces, but that doesn't change the fact that the responsibility of mending our broken pieces is on us. No one else can do that work for us. Yes, it can be easy to get stuck in feeling resentful over needing to do this work in the first place. That's where reframing and listening to stories of triumph after trauma are helpful. It's possible to live a beautiful life not in spite of one's trauma but because of it. That doesn't mean I'm grateful for the traumas I've endured, and it doesn't mean I don't have scars; it just means I now know I couldn't have experienced the significant amount of beauty and success in my life I have without experiencing a significant amount of adversity. This is where the concept of post-traumatic growth that I covered in Chapter 4 comes in.

Once I became aware of the ways I was sabotaging my friendships because I was afraid of getting hurt again, I started making a conscious effort to build my trust in others, but I didn't do it randomly. I first started with people I had pushed away but knew loved me and wanted to be close to me. I told them I was working on being more vulnerable with people and building my trust in others but was scared of being hurt, and that even though I knew they cared about me, it was difficult for me to let them in further. Because they already loved me, and this is what they'd been hoping for, each was patient and moved at the pace I was comfortable at to let them get closer to me.

I started with opening myself up in ways I knew I was blocking me off to them, like with not inviting them to my home. Because of the many sexual violations I've experienced and the many years of feeling unsafe in my home, I'm now very cautious of who I let into my home. It's my sacred space and a place I have control over, and I can prevent people from coming into it. So, I started by letting them know my first step to working on letting my guard down and being more vulnerable would be to invite them into my home. I was open about why inviting them into my home was significant for me. Even though it may not seem like a big deal to some people, especially regarding some of these friends I had known for years, it was a big deal given my history and what letting them into my home meant to me.

Something incredible happened as I did this. As I became more vulnerable, my friends and family became more vulnerable with me, and our relationships flourished. They trusted me even more because they could see I had a wall up and was only willing to give so much of myself to them. After just a few years of practicing these higher levels of trust and vulnerability, I had multiple loving relationships in my life with family and friends.

Part of me feels sad for all I missed out on from the years I didn't allow myself to get close to others, but I know I was just protecting myself. So, I try to focus on going forward and not allowing just anyone into my life, but people who show me they truly care about me and I feel are deserving of a little piece of me.

Yes, there are still times I get hurt. However, because I now have tools in place like self-care and reframing, I work through the ways I get hurt. Sometimes it causes me to eliminate people from my life if they hurt me in significant ways and prove they don't have my best interests in mind. However, I can now recognize the difference between the people who truly don't care about me and the good people who do and aren't trying to hurt me. With the latter individuals, I can talk through how I'm feeling. Being able to communicate with these individuals further strengthens our relationship.

The next activity allows you to begin practicing being vulnerable and allowing yourself to trust others.

Activity

Get out your journal and write down the people in your life you feel care about you and are deserving of your vulnerability and trust. Then put a star next to, circle, or underline the person you believe cares about you the most and is least likely to hurt you. You want to select the safest person to begin this work with. Aim to choose someone who won't hurt you on purpose or cause any earth-shattering damage if they do.

Next, write down how you're going to approach and tell them about the work you're doing on yourself and about their part in the next stage of your journey. Write out what you want to say to them. This allows you to work through your thoughts and make it easier to articulate your thoughts to them.

Then write down what your first act of vulnerability and trust will be with them. Will it be to thank them for the ways they care about you, and you recognizing how you keep them at arm's length and that you're going to try to let them in? Will there be an action tied to it like letting them into a piece of your life they didn't previously have access to? This could be letting them into your home, showing them photographs from part of your life they don't know much about, or sharing with them part of your story you haven't shared before. But start small. You don't need to go from pushing them away to fully opening yourself up to them. You can begin with one piece at a time, and that first piece may simply be telling them you recognize the ways you've pushed them away and that you want to work on that but don't know how.

Write down how you're going to reach out to them and where you're going to talk with them about the work you're doing. Are you going to text them to meet you for dinner or a walk? Are you going to call and ask if you can come visit? Are you going to email and provide them with more details up front and ask for a time and place to get together to discuss it further? Meet yourself where you're currently at. This is a very big step in your healing journey, so you want to make the process manageable, so you don't get so scared that you stop moving forward with the process.

Once you begin this process with the first person you selected, you can move on to someone else on your list. No one person can be everything for us, and no one person can be there for us all the time, so we must build an inner circle of at least a few people, so we have more than one person to lean on. Different people have different life experiences, perspectives, and different ways to help us.

Also write down a plan for how you'll handle getting hurt, specifically by people, in the future. We are all flawed beings and can't always be at our best. We're going to hurt people even if we don't mean to, and other people are going to hurt us even if they don't mean to. That's why it's essential to have a plan for the inevitable ways people will hurt us and let us down. In your journal, write down the people you can call and the activities you can do, like going for a walk, deep breathing, journaling, and listening to music, when you get hurt again in the future. Make sure to practice these tools ahead of time so you can turn to them instinctively in your greatest times of need.

I realize depending on and trusting other people can be difficult, especially if your trauma occurred at the hands of other people. This is where seeking a professional like a therapist can be beneficial. They help you work through your traumas and the issues blocking you from trusting others. This person can also help you get through any rough patches you experience down the road as you bring down the walls you've created to keep you safe. They can be the person you can talk to and be vulnerable with until you build a strong inner circle of people you can do this with. I'll discuss finding a therapist further in the Seek Help section at the end of this chapter.

During your journey of learning to depend on and trust other people, you might run up against your family's inability to be there for you. People often struggle at first with building a strong inner network because as they inventory the people who currently are or should be in their life, they begin with family. This makes sense because, in an ideal world, you should be able to depend on the people who brought you into this world, you share blood with, and you spent years of your life with. However, I know from experience this isn't always the case.

If your family is unable to be there for you in the way you need it, then you'll eventually need to build a new family. Not everyone deserves a piece of us, and this is even true of family. It's unbelievable how many people have tried to push down my throat the idea that I must keep someone in my life just because they're family and that family is always there for one another. I get so angry at these individuals because this belief from my own family led me to being abused in a variety of ways, including sexually, by family. Just because someone shares blood, a last name, or history with us, doesn't mean they deserve our time, energy, or, especially, trust.

Unfortunately, we tend to gravitate toward the same types of people who hurt us. This is part of why those of us who've been hurt by family continue to get hurt when we try to connect with people outside of our family. This is because all humans are attracted to what is familiar. Even if what is familiar is painful, we still gravitate towards it, because the unknown may be even more painful. It's part of why people stay in abusive relationships; it's familiar, and they fear ending up in even worse pain if they leave. It's why many people who've experienced abuse throughout most of their lives tend to be pessimistic and have a negative outlook on people and life in general. Because their life experiences have told them over and over that people can't be trusted and life is always hard, they begin to believe it. Combine this with their poor attitude and actions that push good, trustworthy people away, and gravitating toward people who are similar to those who abused them, people who've been abused are more likely to hold on to those beliefs.

This means you'll need to do a lot of work on yourself to protect yourself from people who will hurt you over and over and to not attract similar types of people into your life. I recommend journaling the things you need from a loving relationship. This way it'll be easier to identify when you have someone in your life who meets these criteria, so you'll know when it's okay to be vulnerable. I do not recommend being vulnerable with people who hurt you over and over even if they're family, because they're unlikely to give you what you need and may never be able to. If you practice being vulnerable with people who will inevitably hurt you, it'll send you backward and make you less likely to get close to people in the future. It might help to make a list of people, or types of people, who deserve your vulnerability and who don't. Write down the people you know you can't be vulnerable with and need to protect yourself from, so you don't let down your guard until you're strong enough to let their words, actions, and inactions bounce off you. I also recommend finding an outlet for your emotions, so you don't get angry or depressed. You don't want to give people the chance to have so much control over you that they can get you to fly into a rage or fall into a stupor with their words and actions.

Journaling is a great way to get emotions out. It allows you to articulate thoughts you may not be able to say or are not ready to say out loud. Physical activity is also a great way to work through difficult emotions. Not only does it release a whole host of feel-good chemicals, including natural antidepressants, but it also releases pent-up energy and frustration, especially if the exercise is vigorous. Dancing is particularly helpful because of the variety of ways you can move your body to release tension and because it's tied to music. Music has its own emotional benefits, so tying it to physical activity, when dancing or doing any physical activity like walking, running, or working out, can be beneficial.

It may take a long time to find people you can fully trust and be vulnerable with, but it will happen. Just focus on what is currently within your control. Focus on what you want and deserve in a loving relationship. Be vigilant for early signs that people are going to hurt you and promptly distance yourself from them. Always remember that hurt people hurt people, and people in immense pain are unlikely to be able to give you what you need. This doesn't mean you can't keep people in your life who are in immense pain. Trauma is coming for us all at some point, so there will be at least one point in everyone's life where they'll be brought to their knees. So, you might have a friend or family member who's typically reliable and is a great support system but falls apart after they experience a tragedy. During this time, they might not be able to be there for you in the way you need them. But this is your time to be there for them. By being there for them, they'll be able to get through their rough patch faster, and your bond will strengthen. Keep an eye out for people who love life, other people, and themselves. They're the best people to practice being vulnerable with.

As I wrote in the activity, it's important to understand that no one person can be everything to you; that's where we often get stuck and feel betrayed because we expect people to give us more than they're capable of. Even our intimate partners, family members, and friends are limited in what they're capable of giving. Instead of shaming or being resentful toward someone you care about for their limitations and because they can't give you what you need, recognize they're doing the best they can and there's a reason they're limited that likely has nothing to do with you. It's probably because of something they experienced years before they met you. Instead, if you want to keep them in your life, determine how you can work with them knowing they have this limitation and how you're going to get your needs met in another way.

It's also important to recognize that we're limited in what we can give others. It's critical to remember that we're also doing the best we can, and that we don't get angry at ourselves or feel ashamed of our limitations. This doesn't mean we can't improve or will have this specific limitation forever, but many of our limitations are deep-rooted, have been around for years, and will likely take years to excavate. Likewise, just because someone you care about has a limitation doesn't mean they'll have it forever, but you can't force them to change. They first must want to change and then want to do the work necessary to change. You can't force them to do either. This is where a lot of resistance comes in relationships. We try to get our needs met by a person who is unable to meet them, and then we get angry at them for not being willing to change so they can take care of our needs. But they had that limitation before they met you, and love is not enough to change a person or cause them to do the difficult work of changing. Think of the effort you must put in to work through your trauma and the habits, behaviors, and beliefs you acquired from your painful experiences and other life circumstances. None of this will change quickly. We may want them to change quickly, but that desire isn't based in reality. The reality is that change is difficult, so even if a person we love wants to change to meet a specific need for us, it doesn't mean they're able to, at least not in the time frame we need. Again, that means we must learn to work around their limitations, just like they must work around ours until those limitations don't exist anymore.

I'm a planner. My days are typically full, and I must plan as many things as possible to ensure I accomplish as much as possible. I've accomplished a lot during my life and have even bigger goals on the horizon. The goals I've accomplished and will accomplish are possible because of my planning, discipline, and rigidity. Of course, being so regimented comes with consequences, and one is that I have difficulty when a plan doesn't work out. Typically, my plans are altered by other people. For example, I dislike when people cancel plans with me at the last minute. They don't often realize part or all of my day was based on the time we were supposed to spend together. I have one friend in particular who regularly cancels on me as I'm heading out the door to meet her. We've been friends for years and, in the beginning, my frustration distanced me from her. As I got to know more about her history and current struggles, I found out she has an extensive trauma history and was barely surviving. I realized that her canceling at the last minute had nothing to do with me and didn't mean she didn't respect me or all I had on my plate. She was just doing the best she could to survive at that moment. She didn't cancel at the last minute because she was inconsiderate. She wanted to see me, but what she was experiencing at the moment overwhelmed her, so she needed to cancel for her own sake. Once I recognized her limitations and that she truly cared about me but was struggling to survive, I needed to learn how to work around her limitations, because I wanted to keep her in my life. This has meant not seeing her as much, but she's still in my life. We keep in touch more through text messages than in person, but we're still connected, and we still love one another. When we do plan on getting together, I don't schedule anything else for that day that'll matter much if she cancels. I also make sure I have a plan B so I don't get upset or stressed out if she cancels. I instead focus on how my friend must be feeling, because I now understand her canceling signals that she's not doing well.

We all have limitations. Ours may be different from the limitations of the people in our life, but we still have limitations. For example, one of my limitations can be seen with responding to text messages, voicemails, and emails. I'm not as limited in this area as I used to be, but the limitation is still there, and it grows in proportion to the stress I'm experiencing in my life at that moment.

By nature, I'm outgoing, happy, and bubbly. However, it can be draining for me some days, particularly when I must strain to be this way. Yes, there are days when I could allow myself to not be happy and bubbly when I'm not feeling up to it, but I continue with the show out of habit, and I know it's the version of me that people most like to see and are most attracted to. However, there are days, particularly when it comes to work, when I must paint on my shiny exterior to hide the pain inside. This is particularly true when I'm doing work that is dependent upon me presenting myself with high energy and an attractive exterior. For example, when hired to speak to a group or a large audience, I can't come in sad and depressed. I will certainly not get re-hired or recommended to speak elsewhere if they hired one version of me but I presented another.

Whether I'm being highly energetic because I must or because of old programming, forcing myself to act in a way that contradicts how I'm feeling takes a lot out of me. When I'm energetic and it's aligned with how I'm feeling at that moment, it energizes me further, but when I'm being energetic and I'm misaligned, it drains me. It's on these days when I'm feeling tapped out that I have tremendous difficulty connecting with other humans outside of my forced interactions. There have been periods of my life where this pretending goes on for weeks or months because of stress. During these times, I'm least dependable to people reaching out to me. For better or worse, I prioritize giving my energy to the people I'm being paid to speak to, and I may or may not have energy left for the people in my life I deeply care about. This means I often look at text messages, voicemails, or emails from my loved ones and am unable to muster the energy to respond. I've gotten better at forcing myself to but still regularly go a day, two, or multiple days in a row without responding.

My current friends and family know it's a limitation I have. They know it's not a reflection of how I feel about them but of how I'm doing at that point. Knowing I have this limitation and why has made it easier for me to accept the limitations in my friend who regularly cancels on me. How can I condemn her for her limitations, when I have limitations of my own —limitations similar to hers? No, I don't regularly cancel plans with others. I'm dependable in that way, but not when it comes to connecting through other modes of communication.

I've also learned that during heavy emotional issues and stressors in my life, some people I can turn to and some I cannot. It doesn't mean the people I can't turn to don't care about me, just that they're limited in that way, or our relationship hasn't reached the level where they're willing or able to be there for me in that way. We only have so much energy, so we can't be there for everyone in the same way. If you're a caring, empathetic, compassionate person, you're going to quickly burn out, and many people like this do, from trying to be there for everyone in the same way. I have people in my life who are extremely kind, caring, and empathetic but spend their entire day being that way at their job and then must be that way for the people in their inner circle. That means they don't have more of that version of themselves to give outside of those spheres of their life. That doesn't mean they aren't kind or caring and never willing to listen to me; I just can't regularly go to them with heavy stuff.

I must be mindful about this myself. Because I am typically high energy, happy, and bubbly, while also being kind and empathetic, I have a lot of new people I interact with wanting to be close to me. I recognize these qualities of mine are attractive to others, especially in a world with so much pain and negativity. However, I purposefully keep most new people at arm's length; there's only so much of me to go around, and I can't be the sounding board and shoulder to cry on at work, in my personal life, and with every new person in my life. That's why I don't get upset at the people I know would be great to lean on but aren't. They only have so much of themselves to give and are already giving pieces of themselves to others every day so must do what they can to protect themselves.

I also know which people I can talk through things rationally with, the people I can go to when I'm fired up and want to let off steam, and the people I can do both with. I have some people in my life I just hang out with and do activities such as hiking with. I enjoy spending time with them, but they aren't people I go to for help. It's okay that I can only experience small pieces of my life with some people while others get to share larger pieces with me. Not only can I not be everything to everyone, but no one person can be everything to me.

As I've become more aware of my limitations, I've made a point to share my limitations with others. For new people in my life, I share my disclaimer at the beginning, if they regularly reach out to me, that I'm not always good at responding in a timely manner. It's a long-standing issue and has nothing to do with them; I'm working on it, but it's something to know about me.

However, it's important to recognize that most people don't come with disclaimers. Most people won't tell you about their limitations, because they're not aware of them. Although I'm certain I have limitations I'm not aware of, I'm able to see many of my limitations because I spend a lot of time in self-reflection. However, most people don't. Most people avoid being with their thoughts because it's uncomfortable. It's difficult to think about your past pain and shortcomings. Most people do anything they can to avoid being uncomfortable. Even though self-reflection can help you move through trauma and difficult life circumstances more quickly, most people are afraid to go to that place. That's why they fill their minds with distractions.

Because most people aren't aware of their limitations, you can't depend on them talking to you about them. This is where a lot of resistance in relationships comes from. Even though another person may not be ready to do the work of evaluating their own thoughts and behaviors, you can spend time reflecting on what they're not ready to think about or say. This is also why spending time reflecting is important. It lets us step back and think about what another person is going through or has been through that could be causing them to act in a certain way. Then, once we can see that the things people do that upset us really have nothing to do with us, it's easy to look at them with compassion instead of anger and frustration. It allows us to soften with others and reduces the stress in our lives.

It's important to know the person, who you selected in the recent activity to practice trusting others, is going to come with their own limitations, so you don't use those limitations as evidence that people can't be trusted and to justify retreating into the comfort of the fortress you built to try to keep you safe. I'm telling you this so you can proceed into this next step in your healing journey with your eyes wide open. Given your fear of trusting others, your mind will naturally be on guard looking for evidence of why you shouldn't trust another person. That's why you'll have the desire to use every minor infraction by the person you chose to get close to as evidence they can't be trusted. This is a common way we sabotage our progress, so I want you to be aware of it ahead of time.

It's important to recognize that some people might end up not being the right person to depend on, at least in the ways you had hoped. This is why you want to go slowly with the trust-building process. This way you're easing yourself into it and increasing your chances of success, and it'll give you time to see if this person deserves your complete trust.

This is why taking time for your own self-reflection is important during this process. When you have the desire to push someone away, I encourage you to stop and think about whether this is fear and old programming at play or there really is a reason you must be on guard with this person. You might not know right away, so proceed slowly to test it out. If the person truly cares about you and deserves your trust, they'll let you move at the pace you must go. We're trying to avoid setting yourself up for failure and barricading behind your protective walls.

When an event is particularly painful, our brain goes into overdrive releasing chemicals associated with the stress response, which causes an even greater imprint of the experience in our mind. It means our brain is going to regularly be on high alert. When another person causes you significant pain, particularly a person you were supposed to be able to trust, your brain is going to send warning signals anytime you try to get close to someone again for fear you'll get hurt again. This is why it feels so hard to overcome; your brain is literally telling you to fear people because people have hurt you in the past. So, you must make yourself vulnerable and try to get close to people even though you're scared. When you do this enough and come out on the other side okay, your brain calms and stops sending warning signals every time you get closer to somebody.

Learning to be vulnerable will take time and a lot of practice. To assist you in this portion of your healing journey, I highly recommend Dr. Brené Brown's audiobook, *The Power of Vulnerability: Teachings of*

Authenticity, Connection, and Courage. It's one of the many resources I recommend for healing from trauma. You can sign up to receive my full list of recommended books, videos, and articles here: *serotinouslife.com/help.* I'm hopeful, over time, you'll experience the healing properties of love and connection.

Trust Yourself

Because most people have a limited capacity for sitting with the suffering of others, it's important to be able to depend on ourselves. However, that brings up a whole other set of issues when we lose trust in ourselves. Just like others have a limited capacity for being with us and our suffering, we also have a limited capacity for being with ourselves and our suffering. It's why most people never expose themselves to silence, particularly people who have experienced trauma. They're always talking, moving, or filling their mind with sounds or sights from their phone, radio, or TV. This unwillingness to be alone with our deepest thoughts is the same unwillingness others have with being with us and our deepest thoughts. It's uncomfortable.

We also push away our deepest thoughts and painful emotions with other forms of distraction, like eating, drinking, drugs, and sex. This instinct to prevent ourselves from feeling our pain is the same instinct others have when we try sharing our pain with them. This is why people can love us and still hurt us, just like we can love others and still hurt them. It's one thing to care deeply for another person, but it's another to sit with them in a puddle of misery. Even if they didn't experience what you have, a little piece of it gets transmitted to them if they allow themselves to get too close to you when you're sharing your pain. This is why many people recoil from us when we begin to share our suffering. This can easily be interpreted as them not caring about us or being dependable, which can lead to us losing trust in them. Just because it can be interpreted that way, doesn't mean our interpretation is correct. Yes, they may be limited in some way and, like I discussed in the last section, we may need to learn to get our needs met in another way if we keep this person in our life. However, this doesn't mean they can't be trusted. The same goes for us.

After experiencing trauma, our natural instinct is to shut the door and throw away the key to our most vulnerable parts, as we don't believe we can trust anyone with them. We don't even believe we can be trusted with those parts of ourselves, which is why we push any feelings or emotions away that even get close to that locked door. The work we must do after experiencing trauma includes allowing others to get close — and allowing us close enough to the wounded parts of ourselves. This is the only way we can begin to mend those pieces that are still raw from the damage done to us in the past. However, looking at and treating our open wounds hurts. Just like a cut hurts to clean and is painful in the initial stages of healing, cleaning our emotional wounds and their initial stages of healing are painful. Many people avoid doing the work, but it's this work that we need to truly break the shackles of our trauma.

I've found that my ability to trust others is proportionate to my ability to trust myself. As the saying goes, "You can't give away what you don't have." This is why our ability to love others is tied to how much we love ourselves and our ability to trust others is tied to how much we trust ourselves. So, if even beginning the work of trusting another person seems impossible, look inward to see if you even trust yourself. When you do, you'll likely end up staring your blockage straight in the face. You'll likely find you're afraid of trusting another person because you don't trust yourself enough to accurately identify whether a person is good for you or not. You might not trust yourself enough to reciprocate love and companionship in the ways other people hope. You might not trust your ability to handle getting hurt. Any time we face resistance in our healing journey, or in life for that matter, it usually comes down to the stories in our head and our own blockages. We like to point the figure at the outside world and blame everyone else for what's wrong with our life, but at some point our finger must turn toward us. Believe me, this part sucks big time. It's extremely difficult when we begin to realize we could have stopped our suffering and increased our satisfaction in life substantially if we had changed some of our own habits, behaviors, and beliefs sooner. This is where self-compassion is important. Yes, changing sooner may have been better, but you likely didn't do it sooner because you weren't ready. However, the fact you're reading this book means part of you is ready. If you finish this book and don't make any changes, part of you still isn't ready. This is why it feels like we are at war with ourselves sometimes, because there are literally parts of ourselves that are at odds with one another. This is why it's common for people to say they want to lose weight, stop smoking, or be more trusting but don't end up making any long-term progress. One part of them wants to change, but another does not.

This is the most challenging work that must be done whenever we want to make a change in our life. To do this work, we must strengthen the part of ourselves that wants to make positive change and weaken the part of ourselves that doesn't until the parts can be integrated. Reading books like this one, watching videos, and listening to podcasts will help you do both. It would also help to talk with people who are on the path you want to be on or will at least encourage you to stay on your new path. They'll motivate you to persist when you face resistance. At the same time, they can challenge the beliefs that keep you stuck in the patterns you're trying to break free from. That's why I recommended in the reframing section of this book that you regularly expose yourself to new ways of thinking. You'll never be able to break out of old patterns until you change your way of thinking. This involves regularly putting thoughts into your mind that are different from your own. It also involves you adopting these new ways of thinking, which isn't easy, because the more different two ways of thinking are, the more likely they are to clash, and the more difficult it'll be for the new way of thinking to take over. This is the same for physical habits. If you go from never exercising to exercising for 30 minutes, three days a week, you're going to face a lot more resistance than if you already exercise for 20 minutes, twice a week. You'll need to meet yourself where you're currently at and recognize your rate of change might not be what you or others expect. When people make drastic changes quickly, it's because their need for change is significantly greater than their desire to stay the same. When people know they should make a change but the need for changing isn't immediate, it's easy to justify putting off the effort. This is why it often takes reaching your breaking point and saying, "Enough is enough!" before you begin changing. Listening to, reading, and watching the stories of others can help you reach that breaking point by showing you there's something more you could be experiencing in life and could expose the ways you're sabotaging yourself. This is also why it's good to expose yourself to different types of people. Different people might be willing to challenge your current status quo. That's because people who are currently in our life know us and are less likely to challenge us. They've either tried in the past and failed, are tired of trying, or feel there's no point in continuing to try; or we're too comfortable with them to listen to them in the ways we need to. Sometimes it takes us hearing the same thing from someone different, typically someone we don't really know, for us to absorb what we're being told.

I also encourage you to tell people about the things you're working on. You must be selective, but telling people about the progress you're trying to make in life and where you continue to get stuck can be helpful. They might be able to look at your situation differently based on their own experiences and because they aren't filled with the same thoughts and emotions that could be blocking you from seeing all your options. If you don't currently have someone in your life you can do this with, this is another good reason to seek a professional like a therapist. They'll see where you're sabotaging your efforts and suggest ways to navigate around your obstacles when working on such things as learning to trust yourself and others.

Trusting yourself comes in many forms, such as trusting your instincts and your ability to depend upon yourself. This includes keeping the promises you've made to yourself. It's interesting that we expect others to keep their word about what they say they're going to do for us and how they're going to be there for us, but then we fall short on keeping promises to ourselves. If we expect the world to show up for us, we must show up for ourselves. This is why these two pieces of work are being done together in this chapter; learning to trust others and yourself go hand in hand.

The upcoming activity identifies ways you haven't remained committed to yourself. Before we begin, I want you to know the purpose of this activity isn't to make you feel bad about yourself; it's simply an awareness-building exercise. How can you hold others to a higher bar than you're willing to hold yourself to? So, if you're looking for other people to show up for you in certain ways you must be willing to also show up for yourself in the ways you need. This is part of why we fail to trust others. Yes, part of it's due to the ways others have hurt us, but part is because of the ways we've hurt ourselves. Even without being conscious of it, we know that if we can't show up for ourselves, others won't either. However, if we begin to prove to our brain that we can be trusted to take care of our own needs, it helps our brain stand down a bit when we let down our guard with others. If we are capable of being trusted, then others can be trusted.

Please be careful not to use this activity as evidence that others can't be trusted. I know some people's mindset will be, "Well, if I keep failing to show up for myself in all these important ways, then others will also fail to, so I definitely shouldn't let my guard down with other people." Instead, look at it as us all being a work in progress, which means that even if someone who cares about us hurts us, it might just mean they're struggling in their own way. They might want to be there for you but are unable to, given what they've gone through or are going through.

The same goes for us. Even if we find that we continue to fail at keeping certain promises to ourselves, it's important to look at why that is versus outright condemning ourselves for our failure. I must regularly do this work on myself. There are many days I get up and say I'm committing to doing X, Y, and Z but, like usual, fail to do at least one of them, typically the same one. For example, I experienced a very tumultuous time in my life while writing this book. It caused me to retreat to some old patterns I had previously broken free from such as turning to sweets whenever I felt overwhelmed, which ended up being multiple times a day. Almost every day, I would wake up and say I wouldn't buy any sweets today, and I failed to keep that promise to myself almost every day. However, during that same period, I almost always kept the promise to myself on the days I committed to writing for at least an hour. It makes perfect sense why I was able to keep one promise to myself and not another. Writing was tied to a bigger goal, the attainment of which had positive emotional associations; for example, the additional recognition and speaking opportunities I would obtain by reaching that goal. I really wasn't losing anything but time by keeping that commitment to myself, but I could see the time spent had a greater payoff in the end than the many other things I could have used that time for. However, giving up sweets was something else entirely. For one, I've had the habit since childhood, and there's comfort in turning to something I know works for me. Two, the taste of sweets gives me a shot of enjoyment, followed by a release of feel-good chemicals in my brain from the sugar. Yes, it usually leads to a crash afterward and causes me to seek out more sugar to get that same release again a little while later, but in the moment, it feels like pure bliss. Because I'm turning to sugar to ease my crappy feeling and am desperate to change how I'm feeling, it's an easy, though fleeting, fix. This is where being aware of why I'm doing what I'm doing matters. It's also why I want you to build your awareness not only about when you don't keep your promises to yourself but also about *why*. You can't change something unless you're aware it's a problem. Even though we may understand on a superficial level that certain habits and behaviors hurt us in some way, most people don't dig into why they do what they do or put effort into changing the habits detracting from how they experience life.

To build trust in yourself, you must begin to show up for yourself, but sometimes that's too big of a jump, at least in some aspects of our lives. You're setting yourself up for failure to think you're going to go from never consistently meeting your needs to always meeting your needs. It's a process, like learning to trust others, and every part of the healing journey is a process. As you prove to yourself over time you can be counted on, you'll have further faith in yourself and, by extension, in others. As you begin to trust your instincts, you'll be better able to make decisions about who to spend your time with and who to give pieces of yourself to.

Activity

Get out your journal and make a list of the ways you haven't shown up for yourself in the past. Did you skip exercising on days you committed to doing it? Did you have sex with a person you said you would stop seeing? Did you quickly turn to anger and say things you wish you hadn't even though you said you weren't going to keep doing that? Remember, this isn't about making you feel bad; it's simply to build your awareness.

Once you're done making your list, examine each way you failed to keep a commitment to yourself and ask yourself, "Why?" Why didn't follow through? Why didn't you keep your promise to yourself? Was there a certain feeling you were trying to avoid? Was there a certain feeling you were trying to obtain? The purpose of this portion of the activity is for you to know what you must work on to begin following through on these or similar commitments in the future, to build self-compassion, and so you see you were doing the best you could at that moment.

Next, identify ways you have shown up for yourself in the past. Even though you may have fallen short in some areas, you now want to show yourself that you don't always fail to follow through on the commitments you've made to yourself. You're going to be inconsistent at times in every aspect of your life, so it doesn't matter if there have been times where you failed to do a particular thing you tend to do consistently. Think about the big picture; what things do you consistently do that provide evidence that you do regularly show up for yourself in some ways? Do you wake up at the time you say you're going to most mornings without turning off the alarm and going back to bed? Do you exercise regularly? Do you primarily eat healthy foods? Are you mindful to catch yourself when saying something negative about yourself?

Now, identify one thing you're going to work on committing to every day. You can increase how many things you work on at a later point, but for now, just focus on one thing. Make it something you aren't currently doing consistently but could with little effort. Ideally, it would be something that would make you feel good and align with something you're already working on, like the daily self-care activity you selected in Chapter 4 or daily progress you've committed to that will help you reach the goal you set in Chapter 4.

Celebrate your wins. You could do this by keeping a list of how many days in a row you showed up for yourself and allowing yourself to smile at the progress you've made. I encourage you to set certain milestones, where, if you reach a week, two weeks, or a month of consistent action, you celebrate in a way that encourages you to keep going. You could get your hair or nails done or get a massage. If you regularly limit a certain activity in your life like watching TV or taking naps but enjoy them, maybe you celebrate your win by indulging in something that makes you feel good — as long as it's not harmful. You don't want to undo any of the work you've done by celebrating in a way that will make you feel bad about yourself. The important parts are to acknowledge that you can keep your promises to yourself and to see that you can make good decisions. Over time your trust in yourself will grow, as will your ability to trust the decisions you make. As you're better able to trust your decisions, you'll be better able to trust your instincts about the people you allow into your life. Your trust in others will grow as you surround yourself with trustworthy people.

Although there are people we need to cut some slack for and whose current limitations we need to learn to work around, there are people who don't deserve that level of patience and understanding. Yes, it can be difficult, particularly when first getting to know someone, to figure out whether or not they can be fully trusted, so we shouldn't dive in headfirst when working on building trust with others. We should first dip our toe in, especially with new people in our life. We need time so we don't recoil back into our shell, and to determine the type of person we're dealing with. In countless ways, people tell us who they really are. But we must learn to trust our instincts and listen when people tell us who they are and the ways they will hurt us over and over. In part, we keep believing we can't trust other people because we keep putting our trust in the wrong people. Because we don't trust our instincts, we don't pull away from the people who are bound to hurt us, even though part of us knows we should. Then, when they inevitably hurt us, we further solidify our belief that no one can be trusted. This is why it's important for you to work on trusting yourself. You'll never trust others until you can trust yourself.

As we know from experience, not everyone deserves our trust. Yes, most people hurt us because of the pain they're in, but that doesn't mean we should allow them to hurt us. This is where people go wrong. You can be compassionate and empathetic toward those in pain while still setting firm boundaries, so they don't hurt you while they self-destruct. Just because they're falling doesn't mean you need to fall with them. You must stay on higher ground to be ready to bring them back up if and when they stop their free fall. Setting boundaries will be addressed in the next chapter.

After we're hurt by others, it can make us feel like all people are landmines, and we can't be sure when or how they'll go off. The issue with focusing only on the ways people can hurt us is that we miss out on all the ways our life can be blessed by letting people in. My hope is that as you learn to trust yourself and see there are others who deserve your trust, you'll experience the beauty of allowing others close to you. It might not happen quickly, but that's okay, because you must go at the pace you're able to given your past experiences and current circumstances.

The important thing to focus on is that it will happen given enough time and patience with yourself and others.

Seek Help

Most of my traumas occurred when I was a child and teenager. In my 20s and early 30s, I thought I had moved on but hadn't. Now, at 41, I can look back and see how my traumas played out in my 20s and 30s, and I still see the lingering effects of my trauma today. Like many who've experienced trauma, I tried to move on without addressing what I experienced. I thought if I started living a new life, my experiences would fade away like they never happened. I eventually found out this wasn't possible. When I pretended my traumas never happened, yes, I sometimes had good days, but then I would have days, weeks, or months when I would get angry and cry over minor stressors, and my depression would get so severe that I contemplated ending my life.

As I started to address my traumas and acknowledge how my past traumas still affected my life, I found my emotions less prone to wild shifts. Of course, I still have down days; life is hard after all. I still think about my traumas from time to time because they're part of me and always will be, but my past experiences don't have the hold on me they used to.

People often struggle to move forward after trauma due to their reluctance and inability to confront painful memories. Soon after experiencing the trauma, or when first addressing it after years of pretending it never happened, you might be unable to talk about certain aspects of your trauma. This might be because you don't remember, or because you fear a flood of emotions might come with opening Pandora's box. Even as people get stronger, they remain afraid of unlocking that door. They may see their life is better than it was so don't want to disrupt anything. They think if they continue as though their trauma never happened, it'll eventually be like it never did, but that will never be the case. There will always be evidence of how it's holding us back in some aspects of our lives. Typically, when someone appears to be doing well but continues to get tripped up in one area of their life, it's due to an aspect of their past that hasn't been fully resolved.

These are reasons a trained professional is useful. They can help you release your memories in a safe environment, give you tools to deal with the release of emotions, and help you work through areas of your life your trauma is still at play. A therapist helped me safely work through the parts of my past I was afraid to touch on my own. Prior to seeing a therapist for the first time, in my mid-20s, I had never had a safe person to discuss my traumas with, so having a therapist who was a neutral listener was important, so I could begin talking about my traumas. As I developed tools for handling moments of extreme overwhelm, I became less afraid of my past revisiting me and became able to revisit my past on my own. As I did this, I talked with my therapist about revelations I had about areas I was still struggling with so we could delve deeper together into those areas. During these times, memories I never wanted to say out loud came to light. Yes, saying things that were deeply painful and sometimes shameful was extremely difficult, but saying them out loud weakened their hold on me. Also, the insights and probing questions from my therapist while I told my story allowed me to change my story. It helped me think differently about my suffering, myself, and what I had done to survive.

If you haven't already, I highly recommend you find a therapist or similar type of trained professional to help you work through the ways your trauma still affects you. Like I initially thought, many people think they can figure things out on their own. However, I found my quality of life improved much faster when I was able to work through my traumas with a trained professional. They helped me explore areas I continued to shy away from. It built my belief that I could handle the pain from my past when I was alone with my thoughts. For years, I refused to speak about my traumas because I thought I would crumble the moment I brought those experiences back to life with my voice. But the reality is that keeping that pain inside allowed it to fester and strengthen. Even when I cried during therapy, I saw that I survived experiencing the memories. It showed me that I didn't need to fear getting trapped in my past misery when I opened that door. It showed me I could peer in at the misery without it consuming me like it did when I first experienced it. Yes, it was painful to acknowledge those parts of my past, and it was difficult to see how my past still lived in my present life, but each time I examined my story, my story changed, and I changed. I got stronger as I weakened the hold my trauma had on me. The same will be true for you. It won't happen quickly, and the process will be painful, but it'll be liberating as you create further separation between your past and present life.

If you've never spoken to anyone about your trauma, I understand that even thinking about talking about it for the first time is terrifying. I also understand that asking for help might not be easy. You might fear being judged or not understood. Although this section on seeking help could have been included anywhere in this book, I chose to include it in the section on trust because it requires a significant amount of trust to share the most intimate and scary parts of your life with someone, even if that person is a trained professional. As I've indicated before, learning to trust again doesn't just include learning to trust others; it includes learning to trust yourself. This is particularly true if you blame yourself for what you think you could have done differently before, during, or after your trauma. This heavy work is difficult on your own, so it helps to have someone lighten the load by easing you into your story and giving you tools to handle the discomfort of sitting with yourself and your story.

Because most people are unwilling to be with themselves and their suffering, it helps to work with someone like a therapist who's trained to be with the stories of others without feeling the need to push the discomfort away. Even when you begin finding people you can depend on in your personal life, it may not be enough; at least not until you're able to consistently depend on yourself. This is also where a therapist is helpful. They can help you mend your broken relationship with yourself. This is the most important relationship of all to mend. It's the incongruence between our needs and actions that wreaks the most havoc in our lives. We say we want to change but then actively sabotage our success.

It did take me a while to find a good therapist. Unfortunately, not everyone who has been trained to work with people and their pain is well-suited to that role, and it can take a lot of trial and error to find a therapist who can be with you and your pain and help you through it. There were times when I wanted to give up and just continue figuring it out on my own, but I'm glad I persisted in finding a good therapist. If you've also had bad experiences in therapy, please don't give up on therapy as an avenue for healing. I've found that most therapists go into practice because of their own painful past, and sometimes their baggage creeps into their work. Don't expect that every therapist can connect with you in the way you desire and deserve. Expect finding a therapist you trust and who understands you to take some time. Expect that a therapist may have to cancel an appointment with you from time to time, including your first appointment, if a conflict arises in their life. If you go into the process with these expectations, you're less likely to get blindsided and give up on therapy if you have a bad experience.

Once you do find a good therapist, it'll help you see that you can find someone who can be with you and your story and not be scared away by your story. It makes us feel unlovable and can make us feel shame when people are uncomfortable with our story. It makes us want to retreat inward. However, it's important to know that their discomfort is not a reflection of you; it's a reflection of the person's inability to be with discomfort. Think of the world we live in. Our society doesn't train us to sit with discomfort. Instead, we are given a bunch of tools to avoid experiencing any form of discomfort. That's why we turn to TV, social media, eating, drinking, smoking, and staying busy. We have a multitude of discomfort distractions to choose from. So, most people can't sit with you and your discomfort unless they've practiced being able to sit with their own discomfort or the discomfort of others. Someone who can't sit with the discomfort of their own story won't be able to sit with the discomfort of yours. That's why seeking a trained professional to tell your story to and reframe your story with is beneficial. They're trained to be with the painful stories of others.

When looking for a therapist, you don't need someone who specializes in trauma or the specific type of trauma you've experienced. There are a few things I do feel are beneficial to discuss with someone who has experience with trauma-specific techniques. However, my therapist, who doesn't specialize in trauma, has been great for much of the work I've needed to do to this point.

Be aware that your therapist may suggest medication. Depending on their credentials, they may be able to prescribe it themselves. If not, they may refer you to someone who can. Some people don't like that providers can be quick to prescribe medication. Yes, some may prescribe medication too quickly, without getting a full understanding of your situation, but many see that you're struggling and view medication as a way to alleviate your suffering.

Medication was essential for me to feel I could even begin to talk about my traumas. I actually asked my primary care doctor for medication before going to a therapist. They didn't recommend that path but were willing to meet me where I was at. I explained that I had a lot of traumas in my past, that I knew I needed to talk about it, but that I couldn't even get to that point because just thinking about talking about it made me waver between severe bouts of depression and panic attacks. Once my mind felt less chaotic and I felt I had more control over how my body responded to even thinking about my trauma, I felt ready to begin talking about it. But this was me. I'm not saying you need medication. I'm just telling you that depending on your circumstances, it may be recommended to you, and there is nothing wrong with you if it is recommended, and there is no shame in taking it. I used to be ashamed and thought I was weak because I needed medication and therapy. That was until I realized it took immense strength and courage to make it through my traumas and now to face them head on, so they didn't keep weighing me down for the rest of my life.

I can't stress enough that if at any point the memories become too difficult to cope with, you're having difficulty functioning in your daily life, or you have thoughts about harming yourself or others, it is critical to seek help from a therapist or other trained professional. I played Russian roulette during the years I struggled silently almost every day with thoughts of suicide. I think it's a miracle I'm still alive because of how severe these thoughts got and how many dangerous situations I put myself in because I was secretly hoping I would die during the process.

I'm so grateful I made it through those dark days, but I didn't do it alone. The next activity will involve you creating a plan to seek help with processing your trauma and breaking patterns that are keeping you stuck.

Activity

Journal the type of professional you first want help from. Will you begin by talking with a spiritual advisor? Maybe you could look for a counselor related to your specific trauma, like a rape crisis counselor, or a counselor or support group related to a specific issue you're facing, like addiction. You could also ask your primary care doctor for a therapist referral.

Write down why you chose to work with this specific type of person or group first. Some people want to talk with their spiritual advisor or primary care doctor first because they want to begin talking with someone who knows them, and they feel more comfortable with. Others don't want to talk with anyone they know about what they're going through and want the person to be a stranger.

Next, write down your plan for contacting this person or finding a person or group to connect with. For example, are you going to call today to set up an appointment with your primary care doctor or spiritual advisor? Are you going to google therapists or support groups in your area? You don't want a lot of time to pass between writing this down and acting. The more time that passes, the less likely you are to act. Ideally, you'll make at least one phone call before the end of today; tomorrow at the latest.

If you're in a place where you can't even bring yourself to consistently talk to another person or group, then at least find a phone number you can call if you're having thoughts of harming yourself or others. In the United States, we have a national suicide hotline, but many states and counties have their own crisis hotlines. I didn't include any phone numbers in this book because my readers live in different countries and phone numbers change over time. The last thing I want is to give you a phone number and have it be out of service when you call. That's why it's important for you to google suicide or crisis hotlines in your county, state, or country. These numbers are free and some even offer text or online chatting functions if you don't want to talk.

If you've already sought help, is there another person or group you can add to supplement this work, like a program dedicated to working through a specific area of your life where you continue to get stuck? It could be a group that specifically focuses on an issue you have, perhaps an eating disorder, promiscuity, or addiction. It could be a life coach who can help you reach a specific goal.

Most of my clients have seen therapists in the past. Many spent years in therapy but can still identify areas in their life where they're stuck. This is where I come in as a life coach. Although we may discuss how their trauma might relate to why they're stuck, we don't spend a lot of time on it. It's been discussed over and over with their therapist, and now they need a way out. That's what we do together; we co-create a path out. We develop a plan for reaching their goals and replacing old habits, behaviors, and beliefs with ones better suited to where they're heading.

Unlike therapists, life coaches don't diagnose or treat specific conditions. Life coaches spend little time going back into your past. Instead, we focus on getting you from where you are now to where you want to be. Life coaches set their clients up with the skills they need to eventually reach all their goals on their own. That's why coaching isn't meant to be a permanent relationship.

Even though there may be some overlap between what you address with a therapist and life coach, the work you'll do with a therapist will focus more on your past to explain why you have your present thoughts, behaviors, and habits. Therapy can help get individuals back to a baseline of good health, as it did when I was barely functioning. And I still use it today to work on core beliefs that developed when I was a child and still hold me back in some aspects of my life.

Life coaches tend to focus on the future and getting you from where you are now to where you want to be. Some of my clients see me at the same time they're in therapy. If the client continues to get stuck during their work with me, I encourage them to bring that issue to their next therapy session to dig further into the unresolved part of their past.

If you're unsure about whether you should seek out a therapist or have hesitations about therapy, please email me at info@serotinouslife.com with any questions or concerns, and I'll be happy to help you in any way I can.

Chapter 8

How Can I Set and Maintain Boundaries?

As you learn to trust others again, it's important to work on setting and maintaining boundaries. Part of why we continue to get hurt again and again is our lack of healthy boundaries. When people have experienced severe or multiple boundary violations, particularly at a young age, it's easy for one's boundaries to blur, so much so that they don't have a clue where the line should be anymore. I've had my boundaries intruded upon since I was a child, so setting boundaries with myself and others has been difficult, and I still have more work to do in this area of my life. For much of my life, I either had such rigid boundaries that no one could get close to me, or I never had any at all. It's taken a long time for me to reach a happy medium and settle on healthy boundaries. Of course, I'll continue to be a work in progress and need to set boundaries with new people in my life and remind the current people in my life of my boundaries when they forget or think a boundary no longer applies.

When you've been hurt and have had your needs ignored over and over by people, it can be easy to think you shouldn't have expectations of others because you'll ultimately be let down. However, you *must* have expectations, or you'll end up keeping people in your life who aren't good for you. I now expect the people in my life to respect me and not put me down. If someone does, I don't keep them in my life. If they're someone I want to keep in my life, I may talk to them about how what they say or do hurts me and give them the opportunity to change. However, the reality is that most people who disrespect me, disrespect themselves and others and aren't likely to change, at least not anytime soon. So, I don't usually keep people like this in my life, even if they're family. If I didn't expect people in my life to treat me with respect, then I would keep people in my life who continue to hurt me, which isn't healthy. That's why it's important to have expectations for the people you allow into your life. It's about setting boundaries. You have the right to set boundaries for what you will and will not tolerate from the people around you. So, I encourage you to determine what you will and will not tolerate from people and practice setting boundaries and applying those same boundaries in all aspects of your life.

Because I don't allow people to disrespect me, I set that boundary in all aspects of my life. I don't allow family, friends, colleagues, my boss, or people on social media to disrespect me. I find ways to shut it down. Sometimes that means I stop having a relationship with certain family members or friends, I might leave a job or file a complaint about my boss or colleagues if they are disrespectful, and I delete hurtful comments and block people on social media who are disrespectful to me. I've experienced a lot of traumas because of other people, and I *refuse* to tolerate any further disrespect from people.

An extreme stressor I faced while writing this book was working for a very toxic organization. Although it sucked the way they ignored my needs and treated me as though I didn't matter, it helped me tremendously in my quest to draw lines in the sand in all areas of my life. I reached my limit when the stress at my job became severe. After a lifetime of people plowing through me and my needs and treating me as insignificant, I finally had enough.

After years of fighting abusers and fighting to survive, I'm scrappy and have always been willing as an adult to go to the mat with people and organizations that are doing something that isn't right. Even so, my experiences with this organization pushed me into overdrive with setting boundaries. This one organization encompassed all the traits of my abusers and made me want to battle anyone who treated me as though my needs and ultimately my existence don't matter. Not only did I start drawing hard lines in the sand with this organization, but I firmed up my lines with the current people in my life. I had had enough and was now willing to tell everyone what I was and wasn't willing to accept. As crappy as it was to experience what I did with this organization, it gave me the final push I needed to prioritize my needs.

Setting boundaries is the ultimate form of self-care. There is no greater way to show yourself love and respect than by saying, "I won't tolerate being treated in this way." The moment you realize you don't deserve to be treated like crap is liberating. I encourage you to give yourself the gift of self-love by determining your needs and setting boundaries to ensure they are honored. That's the purpose of this chapter, to help you create a plan to make sure your needs are taken care of. Of course, it's going to be a process, and not everything will change overnight, but you can at least take the first step in a new direction.

Even though I had been making progress on prioritizing my needs, the experience I had with this toxic employer was the push I needed to take my self-care and self-love to a whole other level. It was like the universe wanted me to practice boundary setting, because, at the same time things had gotten particularly bad at my job, I had two people let me down in significant ways. With both, I set a boundary by saying this can't happen again and told them I can't have a relationship with somebody who would treat me this way.

It was interesting to see how the two responded. One, I thought was a friend. I'll call her Jennifer. She shamed me for saying that I couldn't be friends with somebody who would hurt me in that way. Jennifer said it's part of being an adult and I should grow up and just deal with it, because that's what grown people do. The other person, a family member, responded differently. She cried and said, "I'm so sorry I hurt you, and I will do anything to keep you in my life." It was an amazing experience because it showed me how I can know who is and isn't worth keeping in my life.

People who shame you for setting boundaries and putting limits on what you will and will not tolerate for your overall well-being don't deserve a place in your life. Some people like this will want to stay in your life because they want to keep hurting you, because they feel powerful and in control when they hurt others and can control their actions and reactions. Others might not mean to hurt you but can't help it because of how much pain they're in. However, that doesn't mean they have the right to keep hurting you.

Being able to finally say, "I don't deserve this!" has been so liberating and empowering for me. For much of my life, I've been made to feel stupid, that I would never amount to anything, and that my body was only a vessel for any man's pleasure. Because these experiences started as a child, I felt for most of my life that I didn't deserve to have good things in my life, and I didn't have any right to tell people they can't treat me in certain ways. To finally believe I have the right to say no and don't deserve to be treated in certain ways has been a huge win for me. It's been an immense step in my healing journey, and I could not be prouder of myself for reaching this place. Again, I still have more work to do, but I've improved significantly in this area of my life, and these accomplishments should be acknowledged and celebrated. To finally believe I deserve love and respect and don't deserve to be treated like I don't matter fills me with more excitement than I can articulate. I truly hope you'll also eventually experience the healing and empowering properties that come with making you and your needs a priority.

For much of my life, I've allowed people to cross my boundaries and just learned to deal with it. Jennifer tried to convince me that this is how life works. She tried to convince me that part of being an adult is learning that people hurt each other all the time, and we're just supposed to get over it. Although I do believe people hurt each other all the time, I no longer believe we should just learn to deal with it. She tried to justify it by saying all the other friends in her life hurt each other all the time and don't stop being friends because of it. As I've indicated before, there are people who may care about us and hurt us unintentionally, but that doesn't mean we should never say it's wrong and just keep tolerating it. Yes, we must learn to work around their limitations if we want to keep them in our lives, but that requires us setting boundaries, and if a person continues to hurt us, even if they don't mean to, we might need to remove them from our life until they are well, so we don't continue to be harmed while they self-destruct.

As I reflect on Jennifer, I see she was unhealthy. She hurt herself in many ways because of the pain she was in. There were ways she hurt me in the beginning of our friendship that I never called her out on. I knew they were indicators of more to come but didn't trust my instincts until she blatantly showed me and told me who she really is. I also tried to rationalize why she was saying and doing the things she did. I tried to think of the pain she's experienced, the insecurities she has, and how what she was doing was a result of how she still hasn't healed in those areas of her life. However, she ultimately demonstrated that she was so unhealthy that she would put me in a dangerous situation and would do it again if the same situation arose. I'm so glad I've finally reached the point that this level of disregard for me and my well-being will no longer be tolerated regardless of the pain someone else is in. Life is short, and we must do everything we can to protect ourselves from people who steal pieces of it from us, especially when they show us they'll do it again and again.

As author, life coach, and speaker, Tony Gaskins Jr. says, "You teach people how to treat you by what you allow, what you stop, and what you reinforce." So, we must determine what we will allow, what we won't, and what the consequences will be if someone violates one of our boundaries. You won't typically need to set up consequences for healthy people, because they're likely well enough to understand and respect your boundary once stated. However, people who aren't healthy enough to set and maintain their own boundaries are going to have trouble honoring yours. You must be firm with these types of people, determine the consequences for their actions or inactions, and follow through with those consequences. If you don't have consequences, they're going to keep doing the same thing, because what is going to stop them? They likely aren't healthy enough to stop themselves, so you must figure out a way to stop them. Even if you do tell them there's a consequence, they're still going to violate the same boundary if you don't follow through with the consequence.

Some people think there's no point to setting a boundary, because the other person isn't going to honor it. In this case, you must decide whether or not you're okay with this person being the same way for the rest of your relationship together. If you won't be, then you must set consequences and follow through, or nothing is going to change.

It's important to recognize that you may not need to have a conversation about your boundaries with everyone in your life ahead of time. In the upcoming activity, as you take inventory of the people in your life and the things you'll no longer tolerate, you may choose to speak to some of them ahead of time, but you might wait to talk to others until an incident occurs. You judge based on the place the person has in your life. If it's someone you have regular interaction with, then it's a good idea to talk with them. However, if it's someone you only see every few months, it might not make sense to talk to them until the next time you see them or they do something that requires you to make your boundaries known.

In some situations, you might decide not to make your boundaries known, even though you have set them. In the previous chapter, I discussed a friend who regularly cancels when we have plans to see one another. I never called her out on it or told her I was purposefully limiting my time with her and being strategic about when I did plan to see her. Some people might think I should've done this as a form of boundary setting, and for some people, that's correct. However, in her case, she wasn't trying to hurt me. She wasn't being careless and disrespectful; she was just doing the best she could to survive. It's how she was feeling that caused her to cancel on me, and she already felt bad about canceling, so calling her out on it would just make her feel worse. Also, telling her I needed a plan B when getting together with her would have needlessly hurt her. Again, she wasn't being flippant about canceling on me. She felt she had no choice. This is different from a person who has blatant disregard for your feelings and doesn't make you a priority in their life. These are the types of people you must set boundaries with and make those boundaries known. However, there are others you must set boundaries with but don't necessarily need to tell them about the boundaries you've set.

Even though I didn't tell my friend about how I was being strategic when we made plans together, the way I worked around her limitations was a form of boundary setting. Before, I would get so upset, and my day would get derailed, when she canceled on me, but that doesn't happen anymore. Now when she cancels, I'm more concerned about how she's doing. Her cancellation doesn't affect me in any way that it used to, because I set up boundaries to prevent her from affecting me in that way again. I just set boundaries for our relationship without her knowing. So, I'm now protected and not needlessly making her feel ashamed or guilty about the ways she's limited at this point in her life. It doesn't mean she's always going to be limited in this way, but for right now, she is, and pressuring her to change won't help her get through it faster. If anything, it'll just keep her stuck longer.

Setting boundaries with others can be scary. The fear of someone leaving or their reaction can make it intimidating. However, the reality is that if someone reacts harshly or decides to cut ties with you because you're making your needs known, they don't deserve a place in your life. Someone who gets angry at you for making your needs known will never respect your needs or support what is best for you. Yes, maybe in the future they'll be able to consider what is best for you, but until they're able to recognize where they need help, seek help, and do the hard work of changing, they're not going to be able to be there for you in the way you need. So, if someone unhealthy wants to leave you, *please*, let them go. They might come back later in their life after they've worked on themselves, but until then, it's better that they not be around you, because the longer they are, the more you're going to get hurt. If a person doesn't leave you but acts harshly toward you when you set boundaries, you'll need to decide whether or not they're worth keeping in your life. If they are, determine how you'll protect yourself from them. It's not a matter of if they'll hurt you again. It's a matter of when. As I've said multiple times already, hurt people hurt people. You must understand that it's the people who are hurting who will most likely trample all over your boundaries or be angry at you for trying to set limits with them in the first place. It's important to prepare yourself for the ways some people are going to let you down further when you begin setting boundaries.

If someone tries to hurt you with their words or actions when you set a boundary, look at it as further evidence that the boundaries you set with them were necessary. If any part of you was hesitant about setting limits with this person, look at their harsh reaction with gratitude. Be thankful they reminded you about who they really are and their intentions for you and your well-being. Their reaction might be exactly what you needed to let them go or to proceed with setting firm boundaries with them.

Some people are going to try to convince you it's okay that they continue to violate your boundaries because of the good things they've done for you in the past. Jennifer is one of the many people who I've set boundaries with who tried to prove she cares about me by listing all the things she's done for me. When people do this, they expect that their positives undo their negatives. It's like the man who beats his wife but also buys her flowers and jewelry. These people think small acts of kindness make up for large acts of disrespect and vulgarity. It's ridiculous, but that doesn't stop people from using that argument. So, don't believe the story they're trying to tell you. However, I understand this can be difficult. It's easy to feel a sense of loyalty to people for the nice things they do for you. That's why a man who beat his wife didn't usually start out with doing that. It's typically the opposite. He probably started off sweet, kind, respectful, and even showered her with gifts. He wanted to build her loyalty and make her believe he's a good guy so she'd be less likely to leave when he began to abuse her. He often brings her gifts and is sweet to her after abusing her to remind her of the past times, the good times, so she doesn't leave. Interestingly, these types of people test their limits, so if their partner stays as the abuse, cheating, or other bad behavior continues, he finds less reason to be sweet and show small acts of kindness. He figures, why put the energy into being kind if she is going to stay anyway? At this point, the abuser usually only reverts to the nice version of themselves when they see their partner is at the breaking point and ready to leave, and then the cycle starts again. The person experiencing the abuse has difficulty leaving because they continue to focus on the parts of this person they care about and that are or were good. They continue to hope they'll get that person back or change them.

If you continue to keep toxic people in your life, or people who knowingly hurt you, I encourage you to ask yourself, "Why?" Are you focusing on the good times versus the bad? Is it because you think they can change? Is it because you don't think you'll be able to find anyone better? Do you feel loyal to this person? Are you keeping them in your life because others encourage you to? This awareness helps you determine whether it's time to set a boundary with these people or not and how significant those boundaries will be. For example, will you keep them in your life, but with restrictions? Or will you cut them out of your life completely?

I want you to know that it's okay to cut people out of your life if you think it's necessary. Just be ready for the people who might try to convince you you're making the wrong decision. Often, these people have a vested interest in you making the relationship work. Or, they could have people in their own life they want to cut out but don't feel they have a right to, so they're projecting their beliefs onto you.

I've faced a lot of pressure, mostly from family, to make things work out with the people I've wanted to distance myself from. My family has often encouraged me to keep toxic family members in my life because they are family, or encouraged me to keep toxic boyfriends in my life because my family likes them. I've faced these struggles since I was a teenager when I first started cutting certain family members out of my life. I have family who are extremely toxic, and after being around them, I always feel like I need to shower off the yuck. I also feel emotionally drained and less hopeful about life. They would often say hurtful things to me each time we were together, or they had hurt me many times in the past, and I couldn't help but remember those times when I continued to spend time with them. Yet, I had family members encourage me to keep these people in my life because they were family. This pressure often caused me to try to reconcile and maintain connections with these people, particularly during my teenage years, when I didn't feel I had as much choice to go against the wishes of my family. Of course, these family members just continued to hurt me. Ultimately, I couldn't let them go until I could prove to my other family members that they deserved to be cut out of my life or I was old enough or fed up enough to cut them out and just deal with the onslaught of personal opinions about why they thought I was doing the wrong thing.

If you're a parent, I cannot plead with you enough to listen when your child says they don't like spending time with one of your friends, don't want to go over to a family member's house, or don't feel comfortable around a specific neighbor. It's coming from somewhere. This person has likely said or done something that is making your child not want to spend additional time with them. I said in all sorts of ways when I was a child and in my early teens that I didn't want to be around certain people but was forced to anyway. This means I continued to be hurt in a variety of ways. Setting boundaries for me as an adult has been difficult, because, from a young age, I was taught that my feelings didn't matter and that I should force myself to spend time with people who I knew would hurt me again and again. My family told me what *I* should do to make the relationship work, like forgiving the other person, while never acknowledging that the other person could be doing something wrong. The issue was always put back on me as my issue to work on and my responsibility to fix.

Children and teenagers should be allowed to set boundaries. If they aren't, they'll have difficulty setting boundaries as adults. Setting boundaries is a skill, which means it needs to be learned and practiced. If your child doesn't want to spend time with a certain person, you can ask them why, but don't be surprised if your child isn't willing or able to articulate the reason. They might not know why. Sometimes it's just an instinct they have about a person. Sometimes they don't want to upset anyone or get themselves or anyone else in trouble. Sometimes they're just not ready to articulate what happened. Whatever the reason, it's important that they're allowed to feel the way they feel and not be told the way they're feeling is wrong. If they're made to think that the way they're feeling is wrong, they will have difficulty trusting their instincts as they get older, because they'll continue to assume that the way they're feeling is wrong.

Even if you've been discouraged to trust your instincts, I encourage you to listen to the small voice inside yourself that tells you when something isn't right. Trusting ourselves and our instincts can be difficult, especially if we've been encouraged not to, but we must begin practicing it at some point. It's the only way to begin to feel comfortable doing so. However, even as you get better at setting boundaries, you might find that you have an easier time doing it with some people or in some circumstances than others.

There are still some people I struggle setting boundaries with, usually people in my professional life. They're typically in positions of power. Instead of getting discouraged by my difficulty at telling them what they said or did was inappropriate, I reflect on why I had difficulty. What was I afraid of? Who did this person remind me of? Interestingly, I have an easier time calling out an entire organization than I do an individual in an organization. This means I have more work to do in building my confidence and the courage to tell someone what they're doing is not okay.

Even though I still have a difficult time setting a boundary with some individuals in an organization who say or do unkind and unprofessional things in the workplace, I've at least gotten better at not letting an organization's needs completely take over my own. I'm now more mindful of how much and when I work. I know where I'm heading in my life, and I've decided what is non-negotiable in my life. I know that when I need to work extra hours or during my regular time off, I must ask myself if it will get me closer to or farther from where I'm heading. I ask myself what I'm going to need to give up to work these extra hours. One of my non-negotiables is sleep. I refuse to regularly let my sleep be impinged upon. I know I can't be creative or think clearly when I don't sleep well. I know a lack of sleep affects my mood and ability to make good decisions about what I eat and my level of physical activity.

Every time we say yes to one thing, we automatically say no to another. So, it's easy to burn out when you continuously let the priorities of others take over your own. One area of our life that tends to suffer when we fail to set limits is our health. When we are constantly taking from ourselves to give to others, we get mentally, emotionally, and physically drained, at which point we would do anything to feel good, if even for a moment. We may eat that candy bar even though we're trying to lose weight. We may go out for drinks with friends after work even though we're trying to get our finances in order. We may binge-watch our favorite show even though we have many other things we should tend to. It's so easy to sabotage our goals. However, we're not just doing it the moment we eat that candy bar, have that drink, or are watching TV when we should be doing something else. The real harm was done way before that. These small daily choices we make that aren't aligned with our path typically come from not deciding ahead of time what is and isn't truly important in our life and what we're going to say yes and no to. This results in other people guiding our days, and ultimately our life, based on their needs.

We all have the same needs. Psychologist Abraham Maslow's hierarchy of needs, from his seminal work, *A Theory of Human Motivation*, teaches us that we all have physiological needs, as well as the needs for such things as safety, love and belonging, and respect and admiration.[9] We will do whatever we can to get these needs met. I hear people all the time saying things like, "I don't know why everyone always comes to me for everything" or "I don't know why they don't ask someone else to do it." If someone comes to you again and again, they're trying to get a need met and aren't going out of their way to find someone else to meet that need if they already have someone they know will say yes to them. If people keep coming to you to do the same things, they know you not only have the ability to meet their current need, but also that you'll likely say yes to helping them get it met. This is why we must set boundaries. We must show people at some point there is a line and that we'll hold that line. We must be firm when we say we aren't going to do or allow something, because, if we show hesitation, someone desperate to get their needs met is going to try their hardest to bend you to their will, because they sense that your boundaries are flexible.

So, we must draw lines and say, "No, my needs matter too." It helps to determine what your priorities and goals are. Then, it'll be easier to set boundaries because you'll see where you're heading and what you want and don't want to say yes to. Once you know the direction you're heading, solidify what's important to you, and thoughtfully say yes and no, the people who aren't good for you will naturally fall away and you'll eventually be surrounded by people and experiences that align with where you're heading.

It's easy to engage in unsustainable models of living without even knowing why. It's one thing to live an unbalanced life for a period because we've chosen to do something like get married, have a child, go back to school, or start a business. However, we go into these things expecting we won't always have to beat our body, mind, and spirit into the ground with how much we have on our plate. We expect life will ease up on us at some point, and we'll resume a more balanced life. What often happens, however, is that we can get into routines and patterns of thinking and acting to make it through these difficult periods. We can easily revert to the old ways of thinking and acting, which got us through one phase of life, to get us through a new phase without thinking about whether or not we want to continue living in that way. It's easy to begin living unconsciously like robots. We get up and do the same routine every morning, move through the day putting out one fire after another, and then end the day worrying and stressing about what we didn't get done. Regardless of what your life currently looks like, I'm certain you have patterns in your life you don't question. We all do. It's part of being human. With our big, beautiful brains, it would take forever and would be exhausting to move through every day questioning every step. Routines make it so we have less decisions to make each day, which reduces decision fatigue. The issue occurs when we don't stop to question whether our routines are still working. A routine that works for one period or aspect of our life may not be best for another.

We can even get into the pattern of saying yes to demands for our time, energy, and resources like money and belongings without questioning whether or not we want to say yes. Or, we say yes because we don't want to expend the energy dealing with the person when we say no. I'm asking you to live consciously. Before you say yes to that donut in the morning, before you say yes to that extra work or volunteer project, and before you say yes to going out after work to gripe with colleagues about how terrible your job is, I'm asking you to pause and ask yourself if you actually want to or would be doing it out of habit or to avoid the discomfort of saying no. I'm also asking you to stop and think about what you're saying no to in order to make this yes work out. If you say yes to the donut, are you saying no to your health? If you say yes to extra work or volunteering project, are you saying no to family, friends, or yourself? If you say yes to spending additional time with your colleagues, will you be saying no to the time you were going to spend on a future goal, hobby, or rejuvenating?

It can appear easier to say no to oneself than to another person. This is especially true when we're stressed out and running on fumes.

We feel like we don't have the time, energy, or patience to deal with the possibility of the other person questioning us saying no. However, when we refuse to say no to another person to avoid discomfort, we *always* end up feeling discomfort at some point. Usually, the discomfort comes when we're doing what we didn't want to do in the first place. So, if we're going to be uncomfortable anyway, it's better to get the discomfort over with quickly. If you're not ready to go into saying no right away, practice not saying yes right away. If someone asks you to give up your time, energy, or other resource, you could say, "I appreciate you thinking about me. I'm not sure if I'll be able to help, but let me look at my calendar and get back to you." Responses like this give you time to think about what you'd be giving up and whether you want to do that. It also gives you time to think through how to tell them no.

We're programmed young by parents, teachers, and society to respond immediately to questions, and we carry that into adulthood without questioning whether we should. Yes, if you're in a career where your immediate decision is needed to save a patient's life, then, of course, you must respond quickly. But even if you must be like that in some aspects of your career, it doesn't mean it's necessary in all aspects of your career, and definitely not in all aspects of your life. Yes, people may get annoyed if you don't respond to them right away, but only because they've also been trained to answer immediately and are trying in that moment to have a need met. However, their need for an immediate answer is their problem, not yours. When you allow it to be your problem, you're letting another person's needs take priority over your own. Even though you may not think saying yes to taking on that one extra shift, participating in another volunteer project, or taking on an extra project at work is a big deal in the grand scheme of things, it is. Our daily decisions determine whether or not we're going to stay on track. Remember, every time you say yes to one thing, you're automatically saying no to another. So, each decision you make that doesn't align with the direction you want your life to go, erodes your needs and desires, and you'll eventually look back and realize you gave your life away to everyone else.

Many people run into the most problems with their career. I've always thrown myself into my work, working multiple jobs or going to school or running a business while having a job. As I get older and gain skills, my jobs take on more complexity, stress, or both. Part of me thrives under the pressure, but at times the pressure threatens to swallow me whole. In those times when I can only see more work on the horizon, I must force myself to stop and check myself. I ask myself if I'm on the right path. I ask myself if I'm acting in alignment with my goals. I ask myself what I'm saying no to so that I can say yes to all these work obligations. I ask myself if skimping on something in my life now will even make a dent in the work I must do or if there will always be more work to do and at some point I must step away and take care of myself and tend to other important facets of my life. While writing this book, I took on a new full-time job. Two weeks into the job, I was working late. Right from the start, a wonderful colleague would come into my office and tell me she noticed me staying late and remind me to take care of myself to prevent burnout. Over the coming weeks as I worked more and more, she offered reminders. One day, she said, "Stephanie, you know better than anyone, it's about balance and boundaries." As I smiled and repeated the phrase, "Balance and boundaries," I shook my head at how crazy life is. I told her that the current section of my book (this book) I was working on was on setting and maintaining boundaries. I reflected on how knowing what to do and doing it are two separate things. She recommended that I post the phrase "Balance and boundaries" on my wall as a regular reminder. That's exactly what I did. The moment we got done talking, I went into my office, opened a Word document, and typed "Balance and boundaries." I looked through some free stock photos online and found the perfect image of a woman balancing on a tightrope. With the tightrope representing a line, the image perfectly summed up my new mantra, "Balance and boundaries." I put the image under my new favorite phrase and immediately printed it out and posted it on my office wall across from where I sit, so I could regularly see it. I did the same when I got home from work, so I can regularly see it while I'm working at home.

It can be very easy to rationalize giving too much of ourselves away to our careers or other people. For our work, we can say we need the money, are making a difference in the lives of others, or someone or an organization will suffer if we don't push ourselves a little further. For other people, we can say they need us or were there for us in the past so we must be there for them now. Occasionally, it's okay to proceed with working the extra hours and giving our time to someone who needs us, but it's a slippery slope. It's easy for this to become the norm, and one day we look back and see we're not living our life for ourselves but for everyone else. That's why it's critical to determine what's important in our lives, what we want to achieve, and regularly check in to see if we're honoring our values and moving closer to our goals. We can choose to pivot the moment we find we're moving in the wrong direction. Once we do, we must decide what new boundaries we're going to set or what old boundaries we're going to reinforce so we can get back on track. Remember, we all have the same needs. They may be fulfilled in different ways, but they are the same. So, you must be careful not to continuously work on meeting the needs of another person or organization to the detriment of your own.

In many ways, your company wants to make you feel as though your needs matter less than theirs, because they need to keep the place running. They're heavily invested in making sure you always say yes to them. Many organizations expect or at least hope that their employees will overlook their individual needs for the good of the company, particularly when they have a shift that needs to be covered or a project that must be completed within a tight deadline. As a business owner myself, and as someone who has studied business administration in their graduate work, I can understand why businesses in many ways hope their employees don't have good boundaries, at least when it comes to meeting the organization's needs. However, as someone whose business focuses on helping individuals with their lives, I can see the immense toll this can take on employees, especially because their careers are tied so closely to their basic needs, like food and shelter. This is why it can be difficult to set boundaries with your job, because you think doing so could make you unemployed, and then you won't make ends meet financially.

Always having a financial safety net has helped me with this aspect of my life, so no one can ever exert that much control over me. I know I can set a boundary and be okay in the extreme case it ever costs me my job. Of course, setting a boundary has rarely threatened my job. That's just a fear passed on to me by others. However, a financial safety net gives me the confidence to know I can prioritize my needs. I know many people have difficulty saving money, but that's largely due to a whole other set of boundary issues. It comes from not being able to say no themselves. We will cover this further in the next section of this chapter on setting boundaries with yourself.

A similar thing happens when people don't set boundaries in relationships they aren't happy in or that are abusive or toxic. They may worry about being alone or that they won't be able to make it without this other person. If this is the case, it's vital to work on building your confidence in yourself so you know you'll be okay if they leave. This is not to say a person will leave if you set a boundary; however, they might if they're unhealthy. If they are too unhealthy to respect your needs, then having them leave you might be the best thing they could do for you. Even so, I understand it might be scary, especially if you don't have a strong support network. A therapist or similar professional can help you work on your lack of confidence in yourself, setting healthy boundaries, and dealing with the consequences of an unhealthy person leaving your life, whether they chose to or you decided to no longer allow them to be part of your life. This can be difficult. However, I encourage you to focus on what your life would be like if the people you surround yourself with everyday treated you with the kindness, love, and respect you deserve. Imagine what it would be like to live purposefully, so others get you closer to your goals instead of you spending your days helping others meet their needs and goals. Focusing on these things will help you do the difficult and uncomfortable work of setting boundaries with people and organizations.

The purpose of the next activity is for you to take inventory of the people you spend most of your time with and for you to determine whether they deserve that time. Every time you're with another person, you're giving away a piece of yourself; whether it's your time, energy, or emotions, a piece of you is either being taken by or given to the people you spend time with. This exercise is about determining if those people deserve more pieces of you and whether or not you must devise a plan to reduce how much of you they get when they're with you.

Again, our lives are so short, and we all end up wishing we had more time at the end. When you're looking at the people you're currently spending time with, think about whether they're adding to your life or stealing life from you. And if they're stealing life from you, why on Earth are you keeping them in your life?

Activity

Get out your journal and make a list of the people you spend most of your time with. Next to each name, write how you typically feel after you spend time with them. Do they make you feel supported, happy, and energized? Do they drain your energy and make you feel worse about yourself or suck the life out of you? Do you feel no different, good or bad, after spending time with them? You can use words or draw a simple face; a smiley face if you typically feel good after being with them, a frowny face if you don't, and a neutral face when you tend to walk away feeling neutral.

For the people who make you feel good, decide whether you want to keep them in your life. If you do, ask yourself if they already respect your boundaries. If they do, I encourage you to thank them. Tell them about the work you're currently doing and how much you appreciate their willingness to listen to your needs. As you progress with setting boundaries in the future with people, acknowledge them for the work they're doing to listen to you and how much it means to you. These people are special because we're in a world filled with people passing their pain to others, so we must embrace those who are healthy enough to respect our boundaries.

Even if someone does respect most of your boundaries, there might be a few areas they don't. Or there might be boundaries you could set to improve your relationship. For those individuals, first thank them for the ways they listen to your needs and then tell them about the work you're doing. This includes telling them about the areas you want to set boundaries in with them. Do they do things that annoy you, but you're afraid to say anything? For example, do they look at their phone when you're at dinner? Are they regularly late? Even if an issue seems small at first, it may build up resentment and anger and erode your relationship. I encourage you to be vulnerable here. If you're grateful for them but afraid of talking to them about something they do that bothers you, tell them that. Open communication is key to any healthy relationship, personal or professional. It's never useful to bottle something up; it's going to come out eventually, so it's better to prevent the problem from growing.

For those you're not sure about keeping in your life, decide what boundaries to set with them. How they respond to your boundaries will help you decide. If they're understanding when you set your boundaries and do what they can to not overstep them, they might be worth keeping. However, if they get angry, shame you, and make you feel bad about your desire to set boundaries with them, they might not be. Only you can decide.

For those you know you don't want to keep in your life, are you going to cut them out right away or set boundaries to protect yourself from them until you feel strong enough to cut them out completely?

If you're going to cut a person out of your life, how will you do that? Are you going to have a conversation with them to let them know you're no longer going to allow them in your life and why? Or are you going to stop talking with them and let the relationship fizzle out on its own? You know yourself and the people in your life, so you must decide.

Make a list of priorities. Who should you have a conversation with right away and who can wait? I recommend you begin with setting the boundaries that will be easiest for you first, so you have some early wins. There are a few ways. You can begin with the people who are the healthiest in your life. Although it's unlikely you'll need to set as many boundaries with them, it may be easier to practice with them because they're less likely to make you feel bad for setting boundaries in the first place. You could also begin with the unhealthiest people in your life. Sometimes cutting out the one or two most toxic people, once they're no longer draining your time, energy, and spirit, makes the rest of the boundary setting process, and life in general, easier.

For each person, decide whether you'll let them know you set a specific boundary with them up front or whether you're going to wait to set a boundary until an incident occurs. If you're going to wait, prepare what you're going to say ahead of time, so you don't miss the opportunity when it arises.

Finally, determine the consequences for someone violating a boundary. If you asked them to call ahead of time before showing up at your house, are you going to refuse to let them in and remind them that you asked them to call beforehand to make sure it's a good time? If they regularly show up late for dinner, will you leave the restaurant if they're more than 10 minutes late? Will you stop talking with them if they continue to say hurtful remarks? Make sure whatever consequence you choose, it's something you'll implement. If the person sees that the consequence was an empty threat, they'll continue to violate your boundary because there's no repercussion.

Move at your own pace with this activity. If you're scared to death of someone leaving you because you set a boundary, then set a boundary with the healthiest person in your life first, so you at least practice this new skill. Once you get better at setting boundaries, you should begin feeling better, especially if people used to roll right over you. Once you get stronger and build your belief that you're deserving of more, you'll be able to handle the people who don't respond well to your boundary setting.

If the healthiest person in your life is still not healthy enough to respect your boundaries, then you must find new people to spend time with. However, this likely won't happen until you get stronger. In this case, it'll be most important for you to work on practicing self-care and adjusting your beliefs. If you're in this place, I highly recommend working with a therapist if you aren't already.

If we're constantly exposed to pain through bullying and other forms of trauma, our brains come to expect it as part of our normal experiences. Our brains look out for variations in our normal experiences to alert us to possible danger. So, if your normal experiences involve some sort of pain, your brain may come to interpret someone treating you with respect and kindness as abnormal. Some people feel uncomfortable being treated kindly because it's out of the norm, and their brain is telling them something isn't right. If consistently hurt, we tend to gravitate toward people who are like those who've hurt us because it's what we know and what our brain tells us is safe. That's why breaking patterns of bringing people into your life who aren't good for you and preventing people who are good from coming in can be difficult. You'll be fighting against your brain, which will be telling you that something isn't right. You'll be fighting against an inner critic that might believe you deserve pain and not respect and kindness. After years of ridicule, it's easy to believe all the terrible things people say about us and to think we're deserving of the pain they inflict. The first step in working through it is to recognize what's at play in your mind and why you gravitate toward the same type of people. When you can see that it's normal and even expected given your experiences, you'll have more compassion for yourself when you fall into familiar but harmful patterns.

It'll be difficult to create new patterns, but not impossible. I know from experience. It'll require you to become aware of when you want to stay around people you shouldn't and when you want to push people away who are good for you. For a while, it'll be difficult to trust your instincts, because you're working on changing old habits, but, over time, you'll better decipher between the people you should spend time with and the people you should distance yourself from.

Part of why we allow people who've hurt us to stay in our life, or we replace them with someone similar right after they leave, is because we're trying to fill a void. That's where positive self-care is critical. You don't want to repeat old patterns by trying to fill that void with someone just like the person before or with habits that have kept you cycling through destructive patterns. Identifying a void and working to fill it will be covered in the How Can I Stop Promiscuity? section at the end of this chapter. Even if you don't struggle with promiscuity, I encourage you to read it, because you may have a similarly destructive behavior in your life, and ask yourself, "What destructive behavior do I have?" That way, at the end of that section you can complete the activity based on your particular behavior.

It's also important to know that it's okay if your boundaries change over time. Some people think because they've always tolerated certain actions or inactions from people, they're not ever allowed to stop tolerating it, but that's not true. Any time you decide something isn't working for you, you have the right to say so, even if you accepted it in the past.

When you set boundaries with people, it might open the door for them to set boundaries with you. This is why some people avoid these discussions. We each know we're flawed beings, so if we point the finger at someone else, they could point back. As scary as this might be, these types of conversations allow relationships to grow to another level. Changing anything in our lives comes with a certain amount of discomfort. We can only grow by stretching beyond our current limits. The discomfort that comes with unknown territory keeps many people trapped in lives they despise. I'm encouraging you to not be one of those people. Just because we've experienced hardship doesn't mean our entire life must be hard. Yes, every path we choose in life will come with its own challenges, but at least allow yourself to choose your challenges. Your traumas were likely largely out of your control, which is why many people get stuck after experiencing trauma. They get stuck focusing on what they did and didn't have control over and worrying about what they will and won't have control over in the future. The work I'm encouraging you to do in this book is about taking control back in healthy ways. No, the healing process won't be easy, but it's liberating to know that we control the process.

Setting Boundaries With Yourself

In the same way learning to trust others again involves learning to trust yourself again, setting boundaries also includes learning to set boundaries with yourself. As therapist Nedra Glover Tawwab said in her book, *Set Boundaries, Find Peace*, "Before we teach others to respect our boundaries, we must learn to honor them ourselves."[10] It's our lack of boundaries with ourselves and our failure to honor the boundaries we set for ourselves that causes us to lose trust in ourselves. Trust and boundaries are intertwined.

Just like we must consciously decide what we're going to say yes and no to with other people, we must do the same with ourselves. The same way we often self-sabotage by saying the easy yes to others, we easily say yes to ourselves when it's not in our best interest. This is why doing the work of setting boundaries with others and setting boundaries with ourselves go hand in hand.

As George S. Clason said in his book, *The Richest Man in Babylon*, "All men are burdened with more desires than they can gratify. Because of my wealth thinkest thou I may gratify every desire? 'Tis a false idea. There are limits to my time. There are limits to my strength. There are limits to the distance I may travel. There are limits to what I may eat. There are limits to the zest with which I may enjoy."[11] So, ultimately, we always have to say no to ourselves at some point. What often gets us in trouble with our weight, finances, relationships, and all other aspects of our life is our inability to say no to ourselves. With our weight, it might be the inability to say no to dessert or a drink besides water with our meal. With our finances, it might be the inability to say no to an extra pair of shoes or the newest phone. We face temptation every day in all aspects of life and can't say yes every time. Not only is it impossible to gratify every desire; trying to creates more problems. Knowing our goals and what we value is key to determining whether indulging in the current temptation will get us closer to or farther from where we want to be.

As I indicated in the last chapter, it's easy to point to the outside world and determine all the ways it's not meeting our needs and falling short, but it's a lot more difficult to point that finger at ourselves. This is especially true with boundary setting. We get upset over how people don't listen to us or respect our boundaries but then don't listen to our own needs or respect our own boundaries. We lose trust in people when they cross lines but also in ourselves when we cross our own lines. The issue in both areas is that we rarely take the time to consciously draw or re-draw our lines, make those lines known to ourselves and others, and then have ways to hold ourselves and others accountable when those lines are crossed. We say yes to others without questioning what we're saying no to in our own lives. We say yes to our fleeting desires without questioning what we're saying no to in our life by gratifying that desire. We often do this because we haven't first determined what's important to us. We may have a basic idea about what's important to us but don't take the time to solidify what's important to us, why it's important to us, or what we're going to commit to in order to ensure we're focusing on what's important to us. We expect the people in our life to be committed to us but don't often take the time to ensure we're staying committed to ourselves. I'm asking you to take that time. I'm asking you to sit down with paper and pen, your computer, or phone and start writing these things down. We've spent our entire lives unconsciously being programmed by the world around us and have allowed the world to tell us what's supposed to be important to us so we will buy a company's gadget or service or meet whatever an individual's or organization's needs are in that moment. I'm asking you to reprogram your mind and stop living on autopilot and being driven by the programming given to you since childhood by society and your trauma.

Once you know what's important to you, the direction you want to go in life, and what you want to achieve along the way, you can set boundaries to ensure you're always living in alignment with your values and goals. This requires setting both external and internal boundaries. In the last section, we focused on external boundaries, the boundaries you set with other people. In this section, we're focusing on internal boundaries, the boundaries you set with yourself. Internal boundaries include setting rules for what you will and won't spend time and money on, what you will and won't eat, and what you will and won't say to yourself.

Many people in the United States struggle financially. According to *New Reality Check: The Paycheck-to-Paycheck Report*, a PYMNTS and LendingClub collaboration, 64% of US consumers were living paycheck to paycheck in December 2022.[12] This is fascinating considering how much wealthier most people in the US are than people in many other countries. But the fact that many Americans live paycheck to paycheck largely has to do with our capitalist society. I'm not knocking capitalism because, as a business owner, I benefit from it. However, the various ways big business injects their messaging into our minds through marketing train us to ignore our needs so we'll buy their products. We are then trained to take special pains for companies we work for so we further their bottom line with our work output and the additional products we buy with the money we earn from working for them. We are trained to meet the needs of others. Interestingly, we're manipulated into believing we're in control. We are convinced we must care about social status and then think we're in control because we controlled the purchase, but were we really in control of that purchase? Most people say if they made more money, they would save more, but that isn't true. Most people increase their standard of living as their salary increases, a phenomenon known as lifestyle creep or lifestyle inflation. This is evidenced in the same *Paycheck-to-Paycheck Report*: 51% of consumers who earn over $100,000 per year were living paycheck to paycheck as of December 2022.[12] This need to always make more money to impress people you don't even know or like traps people in soul-sucking careers. This ties in to why many people resist setting boundaries with their jobs. They get trapped by needing a certain income to maintain a certain standard of living.

There's nothing wrong with wanting a high standard of living. It becomes an issue when you prioritize your standard of living over saving money to prepare for an uncertain future and when you can't afford to leave a career that's stealing life from you.

People who are more financially secure are less willing to allow their jobs to control them. They are more willing to say no because they know they could walk away, if necessary. This is a powerful place to be in. Because I've had people try to control me in terrible ways since childhood, I've committed my adult life to making sure I never feel trapped again by another person or organization. This means that when I buy a home, I make sure it costs much less than I can afford. I never want a huge mortgage looming over me and tethering me to a soul-sucking organization. I also make sure to keep at least six months of living expenses in savings so I know I could survive if I leave a job.

I've needed to say no to myself over and over to meet these financial goals. I've needed to resist the urge to show off a big home, fancy home furnishings, and regular extravagant adventures to my friends, family, and social media followers. It's important to note that I do have a nice home, my home is decorated nicely, and I do still travel and visit exotic destinations, but I do it within or often below my means. I always keep in mind the freedom and control I will lose if I care too much about my social status. When I was looking to buy a new home in 2020, my mortgage lender tried to sell me one twice the price I was looking for. Of course, they weren't looking out for my needs; they were looking out for their own.

It takes a lot of self-discipline to not allow the pressure from others to get us off track with our long-term goals. When I bought my home in 2020, I had one friend in particular who gave me a hard time about furnishing it with items from Walmart and Amazon. They didn't understand why I would buy "cheap" furniture when I could afford much better. They didn't understand that I value freedom and control over my future more than I value stuff. And I could not be more grateful that I was unyielding and didn't let my lender convince me to take on a significantly higher mortgage and didn't let my friend alter my purchasing decisions for my home furnishings. The job I had, which provided me with the high income that would have allowed me to buy a much more expensive home and furnishings, ended up being so toxic that it severely affected every aspect of my health. Because I didn't have a large mortgage and had more than six months of living expenses saved, I was able to walk away from the job without having another high paying job lined up. I was able to make myself a priority because I didn't make stuff and the opinions of others a priority.

This is why goal setting has always been so important to me. Not only does it give me something to look toward when life gets difficult, it also allows me to check in to determine whether my daily decisions are aligned with the direction I'm heading. It's why my whole second book, *Reclaim Your Life After Trauma*, focused on the power of goal setting after trauma.

If you have difficulty saving money or want to improve other aspects of your financial health, I recommend you read or listen to *The Latte Factor: Why You Don't Have to Be Rich to Live Rich* by David Bach and John David Mann. As the title implies, it's not about making more money; it's about how you use the money you currently have.

If you don't have good money habits when you're making less money, you're going to bring your bad habits with you when you begin making more money. Controlling your finances is important to give you the confidence you need to set boundaries in many aspects of your life. Not only does it allow you to walk away from a toxic employer, but also from toxic relationships, and to more easily say no to people's requests for your financial resources.

Setting self-boundaries extends far beyond one's finances. Saying no might include not watching an extra episode of your favorite show the night before you must get up early, which is also a form of time management. Time management issues are related to boundary issues. If you have difficulty managing your time, it's likely because you haven't predetermined what's important to you and what you need to do to make sure you tend to all important areas of your life. Effective time management involves looking at your long-term goals, determining the daily activities you must do to reach those goals, and deciding when you must say no to act in alignment with your values and goals daily. It involves catching yourself when you're doing or want to do something that's not an effective use of your time. It requires discipline. Yes, it's difficult to stay disciplined when you feel drained and beaten down by the day or life, but the accumulation of undisciplined days will only pull you in the wrong direction or make you stagnate in a stage of your life you're ready to transition out of. This is about resisting the temptation to seek immediate relief from stress and instead staying focused on your end goal and its significance to you.

Turning off your ringer and notifications while sleeping, working, or spending time with people who are important to you is one way to set a boundary. Yes, there are circumstances when you must be accessible, like when you have an ill family member, or a young child who's traveling, but we rarely need to be accessible to other people every minute of every day. I've gone years with my phone on silent mode, with no vibrations throughout the day, and keeping it on airplane mode at night, and it's rarely been an issue. Really think about it: how many times have you had true emergencies when you needed to be accessible by phone every minute of the day? The reality is that most people can spare keeping their phones on silent throughout the day or at least at night without any real consequences. Yes, some people might get annoyed, but their need for an immediate response is likely their issue and not yours.

If you're afraid to put your phone on silent or airplane mode all day or all night, you could try it during periods you're working toward specific goals that require focus. For example, I write after I wake up in the morning, so I leave my phone on airplane mode all night and don't take it off until I'm done writing in the morning. This is because I know the moment I can see my text messages and emails something could hijack my writing time. If you don't want to keep your phone on silent or airplane mode for any period, because you have one or two people you want to make sure can reach you at any time, then see if your phone has a setting where you can prevent all calls and notifications from coming in except for from these one or two people. If you're not sure how to do this, then ask Google how to on your specific phone, or ask someone tech savvy.

Although it may be important to be regularly accessible to one or two people, allowing every person and phone notification to access you at all hours of the day and night is a perfect example of not having healthy boundaries. Your needs and time are important, and allowing everyone to always have access to you will quickly eat away at time you could have spent working on something important to you, being with people you truly care about, or engaging in activities that bring you joy and fulfillment. Think about how many times you must stop what you're doing or take attention away from the project you're working on or the person you're talking to in order to view an incoming phone call, text, or app notification you just received. All the pings, vibrations, and other sounds and sensations that come from our phone, watch, and other devices can quickly eat away our time.

I discussed the importance of self-care in Chapter 4 and how to incorporate it into your daily life. A lack of commitment to regular self-care is often related to boundary issues. When most people get really stressed, the first things they let go of are typically what they need the most to cope and remain resilient during times of stress. They let go of things like sleep, exercise, healthy eating, and time with people they love. I understand there are only so many hours in a day, and if you have a huge project due at work or school or have an ill family member, it might not be possible to do everything or at least not everything well. However, during your most trying times, I encourage you to think of ways to still incorporate self-care activities into your daily routine, even if you spend less time on them than normal. The reason is that there will always be points in your life where it seems like you're putting out one fire after another. If you aren't taking care of your needs during this time, you will quickly burn out and feel defeated by life. For those of us who've experienced trauma, this is a critical trap to avoid. When we feel burnt out, our past creeps in. Earlier in this book, I equated negative thoughts to viruses that come out to play when our defenses are weak. Our past works the same way. This is why it can become so problematic when we push our traumas away like they never happened, and we try to barrel through one crisis into another with the false belief that we're escaping each insult to our dignity and soul. Pushing away our pain doesn't make it disappear; it just allows it to accumulate with all our past pain, which when it does revisit, creates a flood of every painful emotion. I've seen this over and over with my students and experienced it in my own life. When you're pursuing a rigorous curriculum or going to school while working and having a family, it's easy for the stress to reach unbearable levels. During these times, I've seen students and even myself crumble. It's in those moments that people remember things they haven't thought about in years or parts of their trauma they've never recalled. Your past can appear out of nowhere but in reality was there all along, waiting for the perfect time to be addressed. When we're strong, we're able to push it away and ignore it, but our past knows when we're weak and have no choice but to pay attention. It's like how viruses can lay dormant in our body when our defenses are high and activate when our defenses are low. Viruses know we can fight them off when we're strong but not when we're weak. Our unresolved past works the same way.

Self-care not only allows us to cope with our trauma, so we don't have to push it away, but also to handle daily stressors. Self-care also makes us less likely to burn out and gives our past less opportunity to blindside us. This means that self-care must be a priority, and you must decide your self-care commitments ahead of time. Maybe you'll commit to exercising for 30 minutes, three days a week; getting at least seven hours of sleep a night; or meditating for 10 minutes a day. Whatever those commitments are, they should be treated as such: commitments. That means you'll need to determine what you'll say no to each day in order to say yes to taking care of yourself.

Most people bend over backward to meet the needs of others or to experience a moment of self-indulgence that doesn't align with their goals. This results from either having no boundaries or boundaries that are so flexible that they're almost non-existent. We may justify spending hours watching TV or on social media by saying it's a form of self-care, without actually checking if that's true. Yes, TV and social media may distract us from the difficult thoughts currently in our minds. This can give us the sense that it's helping us. If you find yourself regularly sucked into excessive TV or YouTube watching, reading the news, or social media scrolling, I encourage you to first try a different activity before you turn to one of these. You'll likely find a different activity like exercising, taking a nap, or calling a friend who will make you laugh distracts you enough that you no longer need a form of media to distract you. And you'd have the added benefit of doing something good for your health instead of something that research has shown over and over detracts from one's health.

Setting self-boundaries includes setting limits for the things you say to yourself. We know it's wrong for someone to say we're fat, ugly, stupid, or worthless, yet don't question it when we say these things to ourselves. If you currently have people in your life who say hurtful things to you, I'd bet you also say hurtful things to yourself. Our external environment reflects our internal environment. We only allow people to say hurtful things to us because we think they're right or that we're not good enough to have anyone better in our lives. We think this way when negative tracks replay in our mind that reinforce our negative beliefs about ourselves. This means that in addition to telling people what they're doing isn't okay, we must do the same for ourselves.

Some people have an annoying habit of insulting and complimenting others at the same time, but I also hear people do this to themselves. They might say, "I have pretty eyes, but I have a fat ass" or "I have a nice smile, but I have cellulite all over my legs." We must stop adding the "but" when we're speaking to ourselves and others. Even if others continue that narrative, you must stop doing it when talking about yourself.

Like I've said, we have all these reasons not to trust others, and multiple examples of people treating us terribly, but the reality is we're pretty terrible to ourselves. Again, our outer world is just a reflection of our inner world. So, if people treat you terribly, it's likely because you treat yourself terribly. Yes, someone else may have started you on the path of self-loathing, but no one can get you off that path but you. Again, this sucks. It sucks that others can hurt us and we must pick up our broken parts and glue them back together, but that's the reality of life. Resisting reality won't change it. So, if you find that you have multiple people in your life you must set boundaries with, particularly regarding how they treat you, it's important to first examine how you treat yourself. If you don't stop treating yourself badly, others won't stop either.

Changing years of negative self-talk won't happen overnight, but you can start by becoming aware of the negative things you say about yourself, by setting boundaries for what you will and will not tolerate from yourself. Once you set these boundaries with yourself and honor them, it'll be easier to set and maintain boundaries with others.

The next activity is about practicing setting and honoring your self-boundaries.

Activity

Journal about areas in your life in which you have difficulty saying no to yourself. Do you have difficulty stopping yourself from making negative comments about yourself? Do you have difficulty saying no to foods that aren't in alignment with good health? Do you have difficulty saying no to buying that piece of clothing or doodad that wasn't in your budget? Do you have difficulty walking away from the TV or your phone when you know your time is supposed to be spent on something more productive?

First, pick one area in which you want to work on setting a self-boundary. I encourage you to work on other areas another time, but I want to make sure you're not overwhelming yourself with too many changes at once. Ideally, you'll pick an area to work on that aligns with previous activities in this book, like the self-care, goal setting, or trust building activities, so you see quicker progress. If you start reaching in too many directions at once, you'll dilute your efforts, and it'll appear like you're not making any progress. Continuing to focus on the same area of your life allows you to see greater change faster, which will motivate you to keep going.

In the activity in the Trust Yourself section of the last chapter, you identified one thing you're going to commit to working on every day to start with. For this activity, I encourage you to stay focused on that one commitment and determine what boundaries you need to set to ensure you honor it. For example, if you regularly overspend, do you need to set aside a portion of your paycheck so you don't spend it on anything else? If you regularly overeat, do you need to make sure you drink eight ounces of water before you eat anything? If you regularly speak negatively to yourself, do you need to learn to stop yourself in those moments and say something uplifting instead? If you regularly spend too much time watching TV or on social media, do you need to set a timer to signal when it's time to step away?

Just like how we can't be wishy-washy with other people and the boundaries we set with them, we can't be wishy-washy with ourselves. We can't say we'll go to the gym three days a week, limit desserts to twice a week, or that we're going to bring lunch to work each day instead of ordering out and then find an excuse to back out of each commitment. So, determine a way to hold yourself accountable and write it down in your journal. Will you create a spreadsheet to identify your commitments and track your progress? Will you put your commitments on your calendar and cross them off as you complete them? Will you tell someone you trust or your social media followers about the commitment you've made so you can regularly report your progress to them, and they can call you out when you're not acting in alignment with your goals?

Like every part of the trauma healing journey, setting boundaries with yourself and others will be challenging. There will be times when you question yourself and times where you question if there's even a point to trying to change. These things are just part of the process. Expecting these difficulties to arise prevents you from being surprised and sidelined when they appear in your path. In these times, you must remind yourself why you picked up this book in the first place. Remember why you want to change and how you're dissatisfied with the way you're currently experiencing life. As the common saying goes, "Nothing changes if nothing changes."

In part, we don't set boundaries because we know the process will be hard. We contemplate whether just dealing with the situation as it is will be easier than going through the process of setting boundaries and possibly dealing with the emotional turmoil of cutting someone loose or cutting ties with old patterns of thinking and acting. But the point is that everything in life is hard. Taking action and not taking action are both hard, so we must choose our level of hard.

If you struggle with setting and maintaining boundaries with yourself or others, I highly recommend you read or listen to Nedra Glover Tawwab's book, *Set Boundaries, Find Peace*. She provides many techniques to establish boundaries in all aspects of life and to do so without apology. This last part is important because we don't need to apologize for having needs and wanting to honor those needs, even if the world tries to convince us otherwise so we'll instead prioritize their needs.

How Can I Stop Promiscuity?

Some people, like me, have difficulty setting boundaries once their boundaries have been violated. This is particularly common with sexual boundary violations. Although it may seem counterintuitive, many people are prone to promiscuity after being sexually violated, particularly if it occurred during childhood. Sexual violations often alter one's perception of their self-worth and leave them feeling shame and self-loathing. This makes people seek out validation of their self-worth from others, which may include sex. If sexual abuse occurred during childhood, they may believe sexual abuse is normal and that their self-worth is directly related to how sexually desirable they are. This is what happened to me.

My promiscuity began in my teens when my sexual abuses were at their worst. With each sexual violation, my self-worth further diminished. I did whatever I could to get it back. One way was through an eating disorder. I was convinced that if my body looked a certain way, I would be worthy of love and respect. The other way I did it was by having sex with multiple men. I had it in my head that if a man would have sex with me, then I must be worthy. Even when I knew better, these beliefs stayed with me, as did my promiscuity until about age 30.

My promiscuity was most severe in my late twenties after Stan died. In the beginning, it was tied to me trying to replicate what I had lost when he died. I slept with one man who reminded me of him after another; most were alcoholics, drug addicts, or had been in prison. You can imagine why this never ended well and the numerous dangerous situations I put myself in.

My eating disorder also spiraled out of control after he died. At that point, I was binging without purging, which made me quickly gain a lot of weight. I reached 222 pounds and had high cholesterol and sleep apnea before 30. My ever-expanding waistline fueled my self-loathing, which made my promiscuity worse as I tried to prove that my body was still touchable as it grew.

The part of me that craved to be loved and the part of me that wanted so much to feel significant overlooked the warning signs that the men I was sleeping with were going to hurt me. Even when I did see the signs and suspected pain in my future, I put up with a certain amount of pain to get affirmation from them that my body wasn't too disgusting to be touched, that I was good enough to spend time with, and that I was simply enough.

I knew I was hurting myself by being promiscuous. I knew I was doing it because of the ways I had been hurt in the past. But it was easier to have someone else try to love me than to figure out how to love myself. But figuring out how to love myself was exactly what I needed to do to stop hurting myself by keeping men in my life who only cared about my body.

I first had to decide that I wanted to stop sleeping with so many men. I didn't love myself at that point, but I at least wanted to figure out how to. Before, I didn't want to. Because I still didn't love myself and knew part of me still needed the men for external validation, I knew I wouldn't be able to cut them all off cold turkey. So, I instead kept around a few who were at least nice to me, and I enjoyed being around. I cut out all the men who treated me like I was only good for what I could offer them sexually. Keeping men in my life who reminded me that I was only good for sex, like all the men who sexually violated me, would never allow me to learn to love myself.

Then I began listening to uplifting audio and reading positive books. I filled my mind with information and voices that were different from what I had cycling through my mind. This gave me thoughts of new possibilities for myself in the future and new beliefs about what I was worthy and deserving of. If we were able to change our negative chatter by sheer willpower, we would have done it already. Sometimes the only way to override the negative voices in our mind is by having other voices on our mind on repeat. That's why I'm always listening to audiobooks and YouTube videos, especially when I get into a negative mindset.

During this time, I started hiking alone. I came to enjoy the time by myself and didn't need to fill that void with another person. It gave me a way to feel pride in myself for what I was capable of. I started to admire my body, which made me start to love my body. I started to believe I was powerful and strong and didn't deserve to be treated poorly by myself or others. Physical exertion also gave me an alternative way to release all the feel-good chemicals I would get from sex.

Over time, I started to believe I deserved better from myself and the people I kept in my life. Once I decided that, I no longer needed the men I was keeping around for casual sex and was able to look for a man who truly loved me.

Now it's time for you to figure out a plan for yourself. If you don't struggle with promiscuity, what is a destructive behavior of yours you would like to stop? I encourage you to complete the following activity with that behavior in mind.

Activity

Journal what needs are being met by your sexual partners. Does it make you feel good about yourself, or does it just make you feel good? Turning to sex makes sense because, in the moment, it releases a whole host of feel-good chemicals in our brain. So, the void you may be filling is the need to feel good or to at least feel something. If you're not sure what need is being met, the next time you want to reach out to a sexual partner, stop and ask yourself, "Why?" I encourage you to journal in the moment and delve in deeper by asking yourself questions like, "What am I feeling right now?" and "What feeling am I wanting to get or avoid by having sex?"

You may still decide to proceed with contacting a sexual partner, but stopping long enough to ask yourself why may open your eyes while you're with that person. Then you can ask yourself while you're with the person and afterward whether that interaction was useful to you or not. Even if you think you're reaching out to them for love, affection, or to feel good about yourself, it might turn out that there is something else driving you to keep turning to this harmful behavior. Harmful behaviors won't change without awareness or until you can replace them with a useful behavior that allows you to obtain the same feelings.

Once you determine what need you're trying to fulfill through sex, write down other things you can do instead to fill that need. If sex makes you feel good about yourself, what else can you do to make yourself feel good? Can you take a bath, watch a funny movie, or go for a walk in nature? If sex just makes you feel good, and you desperately need to feel good or at least feel different than you currently feel, then what can you do instead? Comb through your history to think of things that make you feel good that are good for you. It's important that you don't simply exchange one harmful behavior for another.

If you can't think of anything else to do besides having sex, what other tools can you enlist before you turn to a sexual partner? Maybe you could go for a 20-minute walk or do some kind of exercise to a YouTube video first. Even if you can't fill the void in that moment, you can at least distract yourself from thinking about filling that need. Trying to stop yourself from further hurting yourself is important. Doing something that makes you feel terrible about yourself will only keep you stuck longer.

Like all the work we've been doing together, if you struggle with stopping promiscuity or with setting healthy boundaries, be patient with yourself during the process. You're not going to change everything overnight. Yes, you can make the decision to pivot, but that doesn't mean you'll stay on this new path and never slip up. There are going to be times along all aspects of your healing journey when you go backward or get sidelined. It's part of the process of learning, changing, and growing. When we go backward, it could be a sign that we still have more work to do to heal past wounds. When we get sidelined, it could be because we need to take time to adjust to the new stage of our life before we resume moving forward. Instead of condemning yourself for where you are in your journey, ask yourself what you can learn from the times you stumble.

Conclusion

Be Patient With Yourself

Our lives are filled with parts. That's why our life is never completely terrible or completely wonderful. My life has parts that were tragic, devastating, and heartbreaking. It also has parts that have been amazing, beautiful, and magical. We have a choice each day about which parts to focus on. When we focus on the parts of our life marked by pain, we suffer and stay stuck. When we focus on the parts of our life that've been beautiful, we have the freedom to move forward. But changing our focus takes practice and time, and we must be patient with ourselves during the process.

I've seen and felt the frustration in my clients, readers, and social media followers when I'm talking with them over a video call, email, or messaging on social media. They're frustrated by not moving faster in their healing. They're frustrated that their trauma still affects them. They're frustrated by others not understanding why they're still in pain. They're frustrated by bad habits they haven't been able to break. This frustration makes them lose empathy and compassion for themselves and all that they've endured.

If you're also in this place, I encourage you to instead focus on how strong you must be to have survived all you've endured. Practice gratitude for how your coping mechanisms, even if negative, have kept you alive just a bit longer so you can figure out how to move forward.

Instead of looking back on all I did to survive after my traumas with shame, I've learned to look at it all with compassion. I was in so much pain and doing the best I could to survive. Instead of being ashamed of my coping mechanisms, I've embraced them as part of my journey. They helped shape my life into something I'm now proud of.

It's not only important to practice self-compassion for what you've done in the past to survive, but also when you turn to old coping strategies. As I've shared, my life was turbulent while writing this book. Things were particularly difficult during the last half of 2022. During this time, I experienced a significant regression of my PTSD and turned to some coping strategies I hadn't used in over a decade, when Stan died. As a biology professor, I know that everything in life is cyclical and that no process is linear. However, the wounded part of me kept holding out hope that my trauma healing journey would be linear, my symptoms would only improve over time, and I would leave old coping strategies behind and never go back. But none of that ended up being true. It's not even reasonable to think it would be true given how everything in life works. But the part of me who has spent most of the years of my life suffering just hoped I would get a break. I just hoped that because most of the first half of my life was painful that the second half would be easygoing. I got a rude awakening when I experienced this period of regression.

I was discouraged by how I slipped backward, but I continued to remind myself of the wins I was still experiencing even though life was so difficult. Although I was turning to harmful old coping strategies, I didn't turn to all of them, and when I did, I didn't immerse myself in it as deeply as I used to. This is because I had developed healthier new coping strategies. I saw that even though I had slipped backward in some ways, I didn't fall. Because I was using the healthy coping skills that allowed me to climb out of the hole I'd been in since Stan died, I knew I would be okay and this difficult period wouldn't last as long as the others. I knew I would not only make it through this period, but that I would come out on the other side stronger. That's happened every single time I've faced adversity. This time eventually proved to be no different.

During each of the most difficult times in my life, I've not only come out stronger but also transformed, and my life pivoted in a better direction. I truly believe I wouldn't have experienced my current new life, which includes a new home in a new city, a different career path, and a new layer to my business, without facing this difficult period. Even though some days I didn't believe it as much as others, I held on to the belief that I was going to come out better on the other side of my suffering. I told myself I would be able to use this pain like I've used all the rest. I didn't yet know how it was going to serve me; I just knew it would.

Even though I always tried to maintain a positive mindset, it wasn't always easy or possible. It was in those moments that I turned to negative coping strategies. I saw tremendous progress in my healing journey during this time with how I was able to look at myself after I harmed myself. Before, I would have condemned myself for everything I had done wrong in that moment, which would send me on the path of condemning myself for all my shortcomings. This typically led to me turning right around and using a harmful coping strategy again. This time around, however, I was able to look at what I did differently. I saw that I was doing my best to survive in that moment. I was able to show myself compassion by acknowledging all I was currently going through, and that even though I was turning to some old coping strategies, it wasn't as bad as it used to be. I would remind myself of the wins I was currently experiencing and point out the ways I'd improved since Stan died. I treated each day as a new beginning. Instead of condemning myself for what I did or didn't do the day before, I treated each new day as a restart. This outlook also allowed me to combat my bubbling imposter syndrome.

I've struggled with imposter syndrome a lot with my business. Here I specialize in trauma recovery and post-traumatic growth, yet I still struggle. Each time I struggle, part of me thinks I have no business writing, speaking, and coaching people through their own trauma healing journey. I truly believe that the areas in life we struggle with occur to show us what further work needs to be done. Because I continued to hold the belief — really, the hope — that trauma recovery should be a linear process, I think these moments of continued struggle, sidestepping, and backstepping have occurred to show me how wrong I am for thinking that. I now believe I would harm my readers, clients, and social media followers if I led them to also falsely believe that one day their trauma would never affect them again and that they will never regress. I needed to experience such a significant regression to remind me that regression and stagnation are also part of the path of healing, so I can share that with others.

We are all a work in progress. We can't make all our changes overnight. It's about small pivots over time. Instead of condemning yourself for the times you struggle, remind yourself that there can't be roses without rain. Every storm and hurdle along the way is necessary to shape you into the person you must be for the next stage of your life.

There's comfort in turning to old patterns, so it's no wonder we turn to, or at least want to turn to, old coping strategies. It also makes sense that we turn to coping strategies like overeating, drinking, drugs, casual sex, and cutting ourselves; those release a host of chemicals in our brain. Our brain is just trying to stabilize itself. It's important to remind ourselves of this when we're in a difficult place.

I know the battle we fight to move forward after our trauma can be exhausting and feel never-ending, but I promise it'll get easier over time. You just need to hang on, continue to put one foot in front of the other, and remember that day always follows night. Eventually, you'll emerge from the darkness of your suffering. Yes, you'll forever have scars from the ways you've suffered, but those scars are there to remind you how strong and courageous you are to endure all that you have and yet kept on going. Each new level of strength, endurance, and courage is preparing you for the inevitable battles you'll need to fight in the future.

Just like trusting others and setting boundaries with others also includes trusting and setting boundaries with yourself, being patient with yourself includes learning to be patient with others. Most people don't know how to handle going through their own trauma, let alone help someone through theirs. Not even trained professionals have a magic key to automatically make everyone heal from trauma in the same way and time frame. Every person experiences their trauma in a unique way based on the circumstances they experienced before, during, and after their trauma. That means even how you help someone through their trauma will be unique. The people in your life who are trying to help you won't know exactly how to be helpful, so they will do and say things that upset you. If they truly care about you, they're not trying to hurt you; they're just trying to figure out how to help. There's no rule book on helping loved ones who've experienced trauma. So be patient with them. You're each trying to muddle through together.

If you have days where you fail to keep your promises to yourself or don't show up as your best self with others, then apologize to yourself and others when necessary and commit to doing better the next day. That's all we can do. That's the beauty of having a new day, every day. We always have another chance to start over. However, you don't need to wait for a new day to start again. You can either catch yourself in the moment or a few minutes or hours later after you've had time to reflect and go back and apologize to yourself or others if you need to, and then keep going.

If you have questions on the material in this book or on trauma healing topics not covered here, please email me at info@serotinouslife.com. I'm happy to help! I wish you the best today and always.

Acknowledgments

I mentioned a few times in this book that I experienced a very difficult period in my life while writing it. One thing that made it difficult was losing my grandfather, Bruce Lacey. He was married to my grandmother, Martha Lacey, for 61 years. They gave me a tremendous gift by allowing me to witness enduring love and respect and showing me it's possible to experience that in my own life.

I continue to acknowledge my biggest cheerleader and supporter in each book, my mom, Laura Lacey Curler. I know you were always doing the best you could. I love you.

To my sister, Nicole, thank you for always letting me talk, laugh, cry, and vent when I need to. You have a beautiful soul, and every day I'm grateful for you.

To my Aunt Debbie, thank you for always loving and supporting me. Your beautiful smile that allows your equally beautiful spirit to shine through always warms my heart.

Thank you to my editor, Kaz Morran, for polishing my words. You not only made this book better, but my future books will be better because of your coaching.

To those fighting the continuous battle of breaking free from your past, best wishes to you on your journey. I believe in you. You will be okay; just don't stop. Even when it's hard, keep going.

A big hug and lots of love to all,
Stephanie

End Notes

1. American Psychological Association. (n.d.). *APA dictionary of psychology*. https://dictionary.apa.org/trauma

2. Goulston, M. (2012). *Post-traumatic stress disorder for dummies*. For Dummies.

3. Herman, J. L. (2019). *Trauma and recovery: The aftermath of violence – from domestic abuse to political terror* [Audiobook]. Basic Books.

4. Wiest, B. (2022). *The mountain is you: Transforming self-sabotage into self-mastery* [Audiobook]. Thought Catalog Books.

5. Winfrey, O. & Perry, B. D. (2021). *What happened to you?: Conversations on trauma, resilience, and healing* [Audiobook]. Macmillan Audio.

6. Robbins, M. (2017). *The 5 second rule: Transform your life, work, and confidence with everyday courage* [Audiobook]. Mel Robbins Productions Inc.

7. Esrick, M. (Director). (2019). *Cracked up: The Darrell Hammond story* [Film]. Healing from Trauma Film and Artemis Rising Foundation.

8. Brown, B. (2018). *Daring greatly: How the courage to be vulnerable transforms the way we live, love, parent, and lead* [Audiobook]. Penguin Audio.

9. Maslow, A. H. (1943). A theory of human motivation. *Psychological Review, 50*(4), 370–396.

10. Tawwab, N. G. (2021). *Set boundaries, find peace: A guide to reclaiming yourself* [Audiobook]. Penguin Audio.

11. Clason, G. S. (2012). *The richest man in Babylon.* [Audiobook]. Gildan Media, LLC.

12. PYMNTS & LendingClub. (2023, January). *New reality check: The paycheck-to-paycheck report: The economic outlook and sentiment edition.*

Made in the USA
Las Vegas, NV
27 December 2023

83554632R00128